John W...

The Poppies of Troy

Kendall Hunt
publishing company

ustrations by Hailee Ram and Abbi Withers

Front cover image © Kendall Hunt Publishing. Back cover image © Shutterstock, Inc.
All interior illustrations were created by Hailee Ram and Abbi Withers. © Kendall Hunt Publishing Company.

Kendall Hunt
publishing company

www.kendallhunt.com
Send all inquiries to:
4050 Westmark Drive
Dubuque, IA 52004-1840

Copyright © 2021 by Kendall Hunt Publishing Company

PAK ISBN: 978-1-7924-4715-0
Text alone ISBN: 978-1-7924-4714-3

Published in the United States of America

Contents

Introduction

The story of the Trojan War is re-visited here in the form of a graphic novel. Tackling the ancient tale in this very modern medium is in keeping with the millennia-old tradition of adapting the story to meet the needs of new audiences. We must keep in mind that long before the invention of the Greek alphabet, the great tale of Troy existed only in the memories of skilled performers (*aoidoi*) who memorized the text and performed it to music. So, when the first written version of the Trojan War appeared, it must have been considered a revolutionary new way of presenting the story! Although there is little consensus within the scholarly community as to the precise composition history of the *Iliad*, just one of the works from which *The Poppies of Troy* takes inspiration, we can agree that the story is old, *very* old. If there was indeed a Trojan War, it probably took place at the tumultuous end of the Aegean Bronze Age, roughly 1200 BCE. The ancient historian Herodotus, writing in the fifth century, dated the fall of Troy to 1250 BCE, while Eratosthenes, writing centuries later, assumed a date of 1184. The versatility of the story epic tale and its suitability to new forms of narrative—such as the graphic novel—all speak to the enduring power of this epic tale.

The basic structure of the story is probably familiar to all readers. According to legend, Paris, a young Trojan prince, traveled from Troy to ancient Mycenean Sparta from where he abducted his host's wife and led her back to Troy as his bride! The beautiful hostage was, of course, none other than Helen, and, as we shall see, she was extraordinary in her own right. This abduction was the *casus belli*, and Helen's beauty would be remembered in history as the motivation for the Greek invasion of what is today Turkey. Thus, centuries later Marlowe would famously refer to Helen's "as the face that launched a thousand ships."

Increasingly, evidence is pointing to the conclusion that there is some historical basis for speaking of a Trojan War. The so-called Tawagalawa letter, a preserved Hittite inscription (*Catalogue des Textes Hittites* 181) dating to approximately 1250 BCE, contains tantalizing references to a conflict between a group called the Ahhiyawa and the Hittites that focused on a place called Wilusa. With convincing arguments being made that the Hittite terms "Ahiyyawa" and "Wilusa" may be references to the Achaeans (a name the Greeks used for themselves) and Ilion (an alternate name for Troy) respectively, many scholars now accept that there is some basis for believing a war did take place between the Bronze Age Greek west and the Anatolian peninsula.

Certainly, analysis of archaeological evidence continues to verify the existence of a city that fits Homer's description of Troy and its location. While the debate as to Troy's existence and the "truth" of the Trojan War will occupy professors and archaeologists for generations to come, what is undisputable is that the story's thematic exploration of the devastating consequences of war are quintessentially human. In this sense, the story is horrifyingly true: war reveals the most brutish aspects of human nature, and the violence and suffering spare no one and leave victor and defeated equally broken by the experience.

Here then, amidst the wars of the early twenty-first century, this graphic novel enters the discussion. How tragically familiar some aspects of this story will be to readers whose lives have been witness to recent conflicts. How immediate and resonant some aspects of Achilles's suffering, the sack of Troy, and the lasting effects of the war on some its combatants will be. With respect to this, it is impossible to deny the "truth" of this story.

Since the time Homer is said to have recorded the story in verse, probably in the eighth century BCE, some centuries after the events themselves, the great war fought by Achilles and Hector has become the backdrop for later readers to examine their *own* views of war, courage, loyalty, fate, love, and tragedy. In this way, the story is not canonical. In fact, it has constantly been re-interpreted and adapted to reflect the attitudes of the moment.

So, where we have borrowed and changed and manipulated, we have done so with the certain knowledge that it would meet with Homer's approval: he did the same thing, after all! Much of the *Iliad* reflects Homer's own time (probably the eighth century) rather than the actual period in which the war was fought. He wanted the themes to define his story; thus, he worried little about anachronisms. Our interpretation of the story reflects a similar approach to the text, and we take "Homeric-license" at times to sit the story in an occasionally contemporary context. Where, for example, this graphic novel proposes a possible origin for the legend of the Trojan Horse or of the infamous Achilles's heel, it does so in keeping with ancient historians who posited their own interpretations of Homer's *Iliad* as allegorical in places. So too, we have chosen to follow a later Athenian interpretation of Achilles's and Patroclus's relationship. Here, you will find them unambiguously in love, and we hope they stand as examples of fidelity, love, comradeship, and a fierce warrior mentality. It is the arc of Achilles's descent into madness and savagery that represents the truest tragedy, where the great hero's transformation mirrors the effect violence has on society as a whole. We take license with the broader story tradition because that is in keeping with the actual practice in antiquity. Later Greek and Roman writers and mythographers all embellished and personalized the story, so for us *not* to do likewise here would be to do a disservice to the writers of the past. A fair argument could be made that the changing story elements actually serve to emphasize the constant truths the story attempts to elucidate.

You will meet many characters in the pages that follow, and to aid in your reading pleasure and to help you keep track of who's who, we have compiled a list at the beginning of the book. Take a moment to look over the characters in the *Dramatis Personae* and consult the catalogue of Homeric epithets at the back of the book for a list of additional names by which many of the characters were known. These epithets—added to a character's name—were meant to emphasize a particular character trait. Thus Hector, an accomplished and fearsome warrior, is known as manslayer! You may also wish to check the companion website for a guide to pronunciation. Now, it remains only for you to travel back in time and join the gods on Mount Olympus, sail with the Greek armada as it crosses the Aegean and stand watch on the walls of Troy.

We hope you will enjoy this version of the story, and we hope that it also provokes thought, discussion, and even disagreement. If that is the case, this graphic novel will have succeeded. Enjoy.

John Walsh
Guelph 2020

GODS & MONSTERS

ZEUS

- KING OF THE GREEK GODS AND RULER OF MT OLYMPUS
- ASSOCIATED WITH THUNDER AND LAW AND ORDER
- MARRIED TO HIS SISTER HERA (THOUGH KNOWN FOR HAVING NUMEROUS AFFAIRS WITH MORTAL WOMEN)

HERA

- QUEEN OF THE GODS
- ASSOCIATED WITH FAMILY AND MARRIAGE
- HATES THE TROJANS

ATHENA

- GODDESS ASSOCIATED WITH WISDOM, INTELLECT, AND WARFARE
- DAUGHTER OF ZEUS AND METIS (ZEUS' DEVINE FIRST WIFE)

APHRODITE

- GODDESS OF LOVE AND BEAUTY
- DAUGHTER OF ZEUS AND DIONE (A WATER GODDESS)

ARTEMIS

- GODDESS OF THE HUNT, WILD ANIMALS, AND VIRGINITY
- DAUGHTER OF ZEUS AND LETO (A TITAN)

HADES

- RULER OFTHE UNDERWORLD AND THE DEAD
- ZEUS' BROTHER

HERMES

-GOD WHO CONTROLS COMMERCE, FAMOUS FOR BEING THE MESSENGER OF THE GODS
-SON OF ZEUS AND MAIA (ONE OF THE SEVEN PLEIADES OR COMPANION DEITIES OF ARTEMIS)

PROMETHEUS

-THE TITAN CREDITED WITH THE CREATION OF HUMANKIND FROM CLAY AND A KNOWN CHAMPION OF MORTALS

ARES

-GOD ASSOCIATED WITH WAR AND BLOODSHED
-SON OF ZEUS AND HERA

GODS & MONSTERS

THETIS

-A NEREID (SEA NYMPH)
-WIFE OF PELEUS AND MOTHER OF ACHILLES

ERIS

-GODDESS WHO PERSONIFIES STRIFE AND DISCORD
-DAUGHTER OF ZEUS AND HERA

POSEIDON

-RULER OF THE SEA, WHO COMMANDS EARTHQUAKES
-SACRED SYMBOL INCLUDE HORSES
-BROTHER OF ZEUS

APOLLO

-GOD OF THE SUN, LIGHT, MUSIC AND POETRY
-SON OF ZEUS AND THE TITAN LETO AND THE TWIN BROTHER OF ARTEMIS

HEPHAESTUS

-GOD OF FIRE, METALWORKING, AND THE FORGE
-THE SON OF ZEUS
-MARRIED TO APHRODITE

TITANS

-GODS WHO PRECEDED ZEUS AND THE OTHER OLYMPIANS
-CHILDREN OF PRIMORDIAL GODS URANUS (THE SKY) AND GAIA (THE EARTH)

GODS & MONSTERS

GIANTS

-A RACE OF BEINGS KNOWN FOR GREAT STRENGTH AND AGGRESSION
-FOUGHT WITH THE OLYMPIANS FOR CONTROL OF THE COSMOS, IN A GREAT KNOWN AS THE GIGANTOMACHY

TYPHON

-A GIANT SERPENT DEITY, REPUTEDLY ONE OF THE DEADLIEST CREATURES IN ALL OF GREEK MYTHOLOGY
-DEFEATED BY ZEUS AND HIS MIGHTY THUNDERBOLT, THE TYPHOON WAS IMPRISONED BENEATH BY ETNA

AGAMEMNON

-RULER OF MYCENAE AND RECOGNIZED AS THE MOST POWERFUL OF ALL THE GREEK KINGS
-HUSBAND OF CLYTEMNESTRA, FATHER OF IPHIGENIA, AND THE BROTHER OF MENELAUS

CLYTEMNESTRA

-QUEEN OF MYCENAE
-WIFE OF AGAMEMNON AND MOTHER OF IPHIGENIA

IPHIGENIA

-A PRINCESS OF MYCENAE AND YOUNG DAUGHTER OF AGAMEMNON AND CLYTEMNESTRA

THE GREEKS

MENELAUS

-KING OF SPARTA AND HUSBAND OF HELEN
-BROTHER OF AGAMEMNON

HELEN

-QUEEN OF SPARTA AND WIFE OF MENELAUS

ODYSSEUS

-KING OF ITHACA
-HUSBAND OF PENELOPE AND FATHER OF TELEMACHUS
-KNOWN AS A GREAT SPEAKER AND A CUNNING AND WILY TRICKSTER

PENELOPE

-QUEEN OF ITHACA
-WIFE TO ODYSSEUS AND MOTHER OF TELEMACHUS

TELEMACHUS

-PRINCE OF ITHACA AND INFANT SON OF ODYSSEUS AND PENELOPE

NESTOR

-KING OF PYLOS
-KNOWN FOR HIS WISDOM AND SAGE COUNSEL

THE GREEKS

PELEUS

-FATHER OF ACHILLES AND HUSBAND OF THETIS

ACHILLES

-KING AND LEADER OF THE MYRMIDONS
-A LEGENDARY HERO AND THE GREATEST OF ALL THE GREEK WARRIORS
-SON OF THETIS AND PELEUS

PATROCLUS

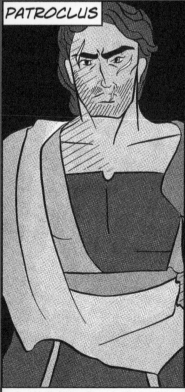

-A MYRMIDON SOLDIER WHO ACCOMPANIES ACHILLES TO TROY

AJAX

-A GREEK HERO FROM SALAMIS
-KNOWN AS AJAX THE GREAT DUE TO HIS TOWERING FIGURE, AS WELL AS HIS HUGE SHIELD
-RESPECTED FOR HIS COURAGE AND HONOR

DIOMEDES

-A GREEK HERO FROM ARGOS
-A FAVORITE OR ATHENA, AND SECOND ONLY TO ACHILLES FOR PROWESS IN BATTLE

PHILOCTETES

-A GREEK HERO FAMED FOR HIS ARCHERY AND MIGHTY BOW WHICH ONCE BELONGED TO HERAKLES HIMSELF

THE GREEKS

PROTESILAUS

-A GREEK HERO FROM PHYLAKE IN PHTHIOTIS, HE HAD ONCE COMPETED FOR HELEN'S HAND IN MARRIAGE

PALAMEDES

-HERALD OF AGAMEMNON, KING OF MYCENAE

LEDA

-MOTHER OF HELEN AND ONE OF ZEUS' MORTAL "CONQUESTS"

—ODYSSEUS' BEST SPY

—CAPTAIN OF ACHILLES'
MYRMIDONS

THE GREEKS

PRIAM

—KING OF TROY AND FATHER TO HECTOR AND PARIS

HECUBA

—QUEEN OF TROY AND MOTHER TO HECTOR AND PARIS

HECTOR

—A PRINCE OF TROY AND HUSBAND TO ANDROMACHE
—ONE OF THE LEADERS OF THE TROJAN ARMY
—CALLED THE "MAN-SLAYER", HE IS FAMED AS THE GREATEST TROJAN WARRIOR

THE TROJANS

ANDROMACHE

—A PRINCESS OF TROY, WIFE OF HECTOR, AND MOTHER OF ASTYANAX

ASTYANAX

—A PRINCE OF TROY AND CHILD OF HECTOR AND ANDROMACHE

PARIS

—A PRINCE OF TROY (ORIGINALLY) ABANDONED AS A CHILD BUT LATER RETURNS TO RE-JOIN THE ROYAL FAMILY

PENTHESILEA

-QUEEN OF THE AMAZONS,
-THE AMAZONS ARE ALLIES OF TROY

MYRINA

-CAPTAIN OF THE AMAZONS

MEMNON

-KING OF THE ETHIOPIANS AND SON OF THE GODDESS OF DAWN
-THE ETHIOPIANS ARE ALLIES OF TROY

THE TROJANS

AGELAUS

-A SHEPHERD AND TRUSTED SERVANT OF PRIAM

DEIPHOBUS

-A PRINCE OF TROY
-AMONG THE TROJANS HE IS A NOTED WARRIOR OF GREAT SKILL

CHAPTER ONE

THUNDER ON OLYMPUS

ANCIENT GREECE

MACEDONIA

MT OLYMPUS

THESSALY

PHTHIOTIS

PHTHIA

AEGEAN SEA

TENEDOS

TROY

MT IDA

PHRYGIA

LYDIA

CARIA

AULIS

DELPHI

ATHENS

ITHACA

ACHAEA

MYCENAE

ARGOS

SALAMIS

AEGINA

ARCADIA

SPARTA

LACONIA

PYLOS

CRETE

N

E

3000 YEARS AGO, A GREAT AND TERRIBLE WAR WAS FOUGHT ON THE SHORES OF THE AEGEAN. A COALITION OF GREEKS SAILED EAST TO SACK THE CITY OF TROY. SOME SAY THE WAR WAS FOUGHT FOR LOVE, WHILE FOR OTHERS, GREED WAS THE REAL MOTIVE. WHATEVER THE CAUSE, WAR, IT SEEMS, IS A TRAGEDY AS OLD AS THE STORY OF HUMANITY ITSELF.

AS OUR STORY OPENS, THE GREAT CITY OF TROY LAYS A SMOLDERING RUIN. THE REMAINS OF A HORSE STAND OUT AGAINST THE APOCALYPTIC BACKDROP.

THE SEEDS OF THIS TRAGEDY WERE SOWN YEARS BEFORE WHEN POWERFUL FORCES ON MT OLYMPUS BEYOND HUMAN RECKONING, DECIDED THE FATES OF COUNTLESS MORTALS.

FROM THE TOPS OF MT OLYMPUS, ZEUS – GREATEST OF THE OLYMPIAN GODS – THUNDERED HIS RAGE AT MORTALS. THOUGH HE IS HESITANT TO GIVE VOICE TO HIS FEAR THAT IF HUMANS CEASE TO WORSHIP THE GODS, THE GODS WILL FADE AWAY, HE UNLEASHES A PLAN TO PUNISH HUMANKIND AND SECURE THE FUTURE OF THE PANTHEON.

HERMES, THE TRICKSTER-GOD, WHISPERED AN IDEA INTO HIS DIVINE FATHER'S EAR.

YOU COULD USE THE WEDDING OF PELEUS AND THETIS...

SOME THINGS NEVER CHANGE. ALL WARS NEED AN EXCUSE.

PERFECT. THE WAR WILL START AT THE WEDDING!

HERA, ZEUS' WIFE, WORRIED LITTLE ABOUT HUMAN SUFFERING.

APOLLO, ZEUS' SON, MURMURED HIS ASSENT ALONG WITH THE OTHER OLYMPIANS.

AN INTERESTING PROPOSITION

MORE SOULS FOR HADES, MY DEAR PERSEPHONE.

FOR ALTHOUGH SOME LOVED THE TROJANS AND OTHERS THE GREEKS, THEY FEARED ZEUS' WRATH

KILL THEM ALL!

FATHER... JUST WHAT ARE YOU PLANNING...

THREE POWERFUL GODDESSES VIE FOR THE APPLE. EACH BELIEVES HERSELF TO BE WORTHY OF THE TITLE "MOST BEAUTIFUL".

I AM ATHENA, ZEUS' DAUGHTER, THE VIRGIN-GODDESS OF WISDOM AND WARFARE. ALL OF ATHENS WORSHIPS ME. THE APPLE IS MINE!

I AM APHRODITE, THE GODDESS OF LOVE. THE APPLE IS OBVIOUSLY FOR ME!

DOWN, BOTH OF YOU! I AM HERA, QUEEN OF THE GODS. ZEUS, HUSBAND! GIVE THE APPLE TO ME!

CHAPTER TWO

A PRODICAL SON

IN THE TWILIGHT YEARS OF THE BRONZE AGE, TROY IS THE MOST GLORIOUS, COSMOPOLITAN, AND PROSPEROUS CITY IN THE AEGEAN WORLD. ACCORDING TO LEGEND, ITS IMPREGNABLE DEFENSIVE WALLS HAD BEEN BUILT BY THE GODS APOLLO AND POSEIDON. THE CITY WAS RULED BY NOBLE, OLD KING PRIAM, WHO SAT UPON THE THRONE WITH HIS WIFE, HECUBA. THEY HAD MANY CHILDREN TOGETHER, AND, BY THE BLESSING OF THE GODS, HECUBA WAS PREGNANT AGAIN. LITTLE DID SHE REALIZE, HOWEVER, THAT SHE CARRIED THE DOOM OF THE CITY WITHIN HER WOMB... LET US TURN TO THE ROYAL PALACE.

AS QUEEN HECUBA SLEPT ONE NIGHT, PREGNANT WITH THE FUTURE PRINCE PARIS, SHE HAD A DISTURBING DREAM.

SHE GIVES BIRTH TO A SON...

...AS HER KINGDOM BURNS AROUND HER.

THE NEXT MORNING THE PALACE SEER AESACUS INTERPRETED THE DREAM FOR THE KING AND QUEEN.

IT'S A BAD OMEN, MY QUEEN...

YOU MUST KILL THIS CHILD!

21

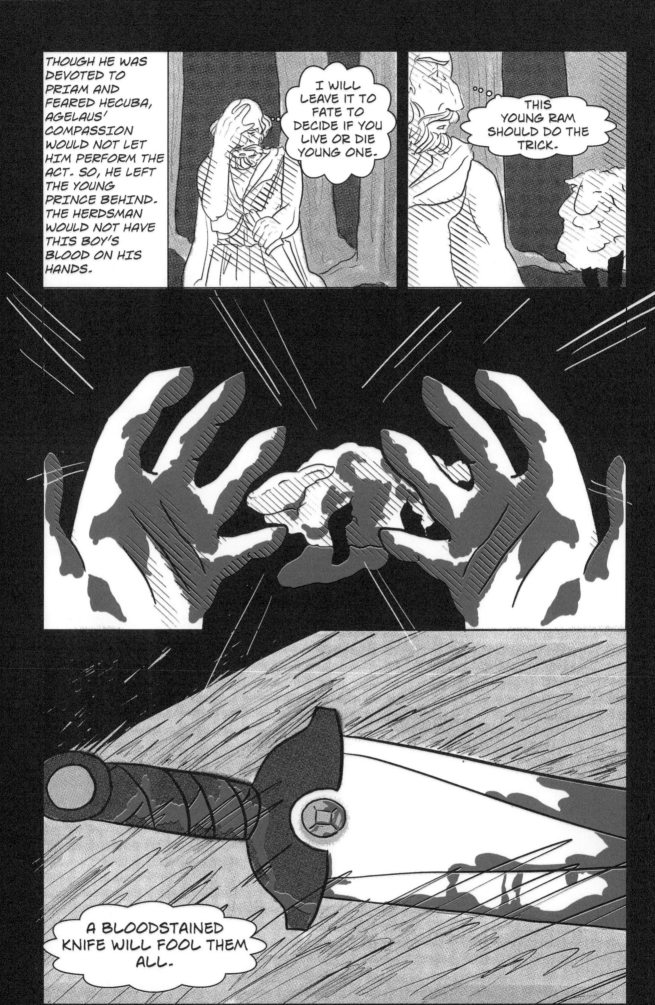

THE CRIES OF THE TERRIFIED INFANT ECHOED THROUGHOUT THE FOREST, ATTRACTING THE ATTENTION OF A HUNGRY SHE-BEAR; DRAWN BY THE WAILING, SHE APPROACHED THE EASY MEAL WITH GAPING JAWS.

WAAAAARAH WAHAABAAAH

BUT FATE WAS NOT FINISHED WITH TINY PARIS, NOR IS IT SO EASILY CAST ASIDE BY THE EFFORTS OF MERE MORTALS. HECUBA'S DREADFUL PREMONITION COULD NOT BE FORESTALLED AND THE BEAR NUZZLED THE CHILD SAFELY.

PARIS IS DISCOVERED BY SHEPHERDS. BITTER IRONY! THEY WILL SAVE THIS ONE CHILD AND UNWITTINGLY SEAL THE DOOM OF THOUSANDS.

BY THE GODS! IT'S A CHILD, AND HE LIVES!

HECUBA WRESTLES WITH HER CONSCIENCE.

ANDROMACHE, YOU'RE A MOTHER. YOU KNOW HOW HARD IT WAS FOR ME... HE WAS SO LITTLE...

WE ALL THOUGHT YOU WERE SO BRAVE WHEN WE LEARNED WHAT YOU AND PRIAM HAD DONE FOR THE CITY... BUT NOW MY HUSBAND HAS A NEW BROTHER. MAYBE FATE WAS TESTING YOU—

YES, IT WAS. AND WE FAILED.

AT FIRST, THE FEAR THAT ACCOMPANIED PARIS' RETURN APPEARED TO HAVE BEEN PREMATURE. THE HANDSOME PRINCE IS SOON BELOVED BY THE TROJANS—PARTICULARLY THE YOUNG WOMEN OF TROY, WHO FIND THE PRINCE IRRESISTIBLE.

CHAPTER THREE

FRUIT OF THE POISONOUS TREE

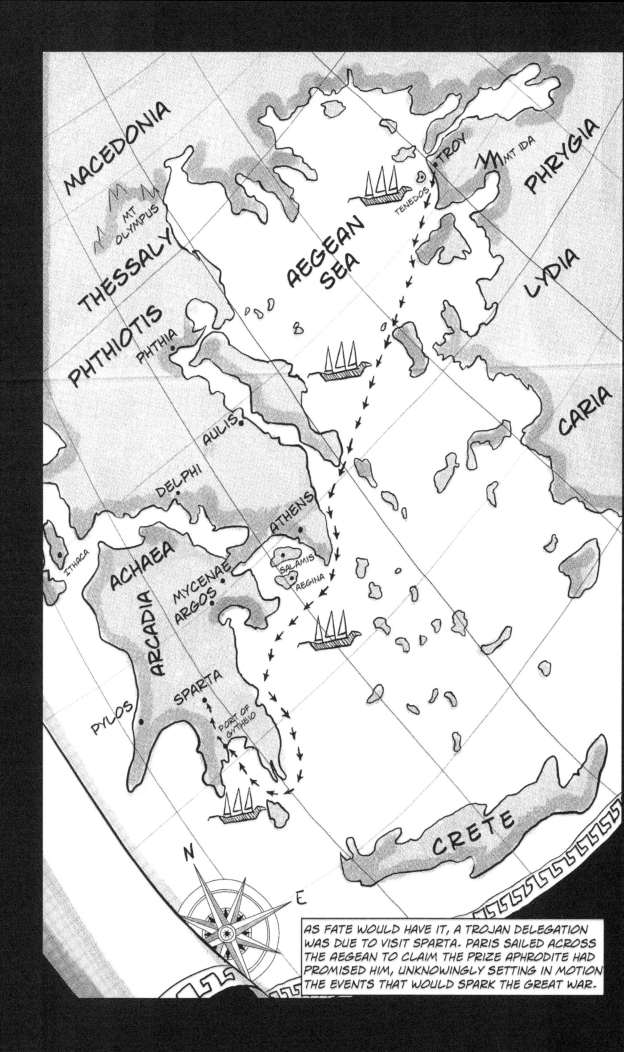

AS FATE WOULD HAVE IT, A TROJAN DELEGATION WAS DUE TO VISIT SPARTA. PARIS SAILED ACROSS THE AEGEAN TO CLAIM THE PRIZE APHRODITE HAD PROMISED HIM, UNKNOWINGLY SETTING IN MOTION THE EVENTS THAT WOULD SPARK THE GREAT WAR.

CHAPTER FOUR

HEARTFELT WOUNDS

MENELAUS TELLS PARIS HELEN'S STORY. HE BEGAN WITH ZEUS, WHO, AS USUAL, LUSTED AFTER A MORTAL WOMAN — LEDA.

IN ORDER TO HAVE HIS WAY WITH HER, ZEUS DISGUISED HIMSELF AS A SWAN.

NOW, HELEN'S RENOWNED BEAUTY WAS A PROBLEM FOR HER PARENTS. IT ATTRACTED POWERFUL MEN WHO WANTED TO POSSESS HER, TO OWN HER.

AS A CHILD, SHE'D BEEN KIDNAPPED BY NONE OTHER THAN THESEUS, THE ATHENIAN HERO.

AND LATER, THE GREAT KINGS OF GREECE FOUGHT OVER HER

TO END THE CONFLICT, AFTER A GREAT COUNCIL...

HELEN SELECTED MENELAUS – KING OF SPARTA – TO BE HER HUSBAND.

THE OATH WAS BOUND WITH A SACRIFICE OF A HORSE.

MY BRIDE, CERTAINLY A WELL-DESERVED PRIZE.

I'M DOING THIS TO AVOID A NEEDLESS WAR.

NO ONE SHOULD EVER HAVE TO DIE IN MY NAME.

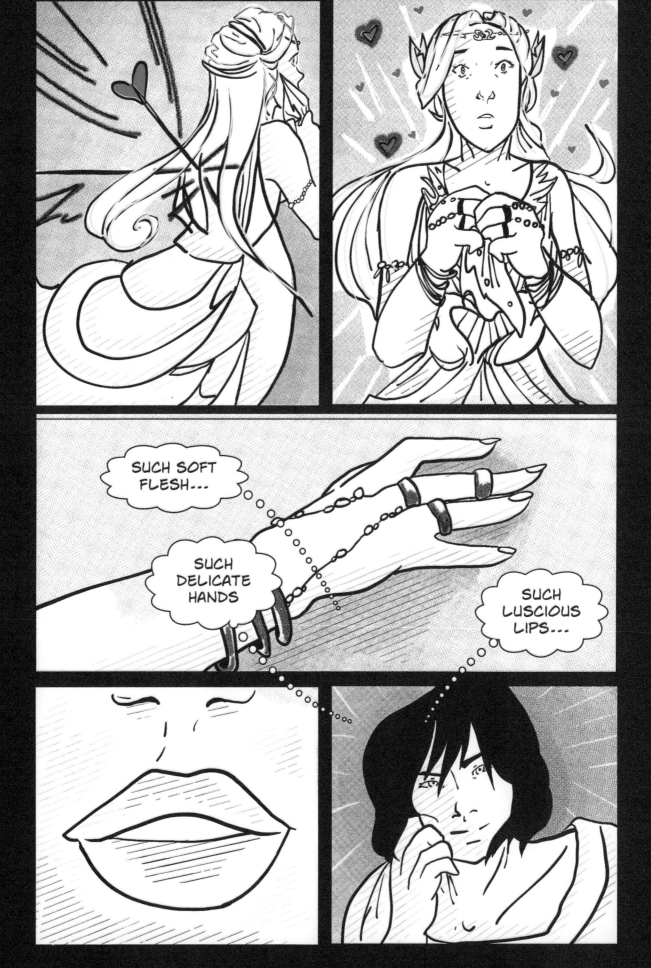

55

AND THUS, ONCE AGAIN SOLDIERS ARE CALLED TO BLEED FOR THE WOUNDED EGOS OF KINGS.

CHAPTER FIVE

THE GATHERING STORM

KING MENELAUS TRAVELS FROM SPARTA TO MYCENAE, SEAT OF POWER OF AGAMEMNON, THE MOST POWERFUL OF THE GREEK KINGS.

AULIS

DELPHI

ATHENS

ACHAEA

MYCENAE

ARGOS

SALAMIS

ARCADIA

PYLOS

SPARTA

LACONIA

N

E

AFTER COMPLETING THE JOURNEY TO MYCENAE, MENELAUS APPROACHES THE FABLED LION GATE, THE ENTRYWAY TO THE FORMIDABLE CITADEL AND SEAT OF HIS BROTHER AGAMEMNON'S POWER.

HAIL, BROTHER!

HAIL!

WITH GREAT FURY, MENELAUS RECOUNTS TO HIS BROTHER HOW PARIS FLAUNTED HIS OBLIGATIONS AS A GUEST AND STOLE HELEN, HIS WIFE, AND STOLE HIS HONOR.

WHERE MENELAUS SEES A SLIGHT, AGAMEMNON SEES AN OPPORTUNITY.

WHO DO THESE TROJANS THINK THEY ARE, TO SPIT IN MY FACE!

AT LAST— AN EXCUSE TO CONQUER TROY!

WHO ARE THEY INDEED, BROTHER! TELL ME MORE...

I CAN USE THIS MESS TO BRING THE OTHER GREEK KINGS ON BOARD.

THEY INSULT NOT JUST YOU BROTHER, NOT JUST SPARTA, BUT EVERY GREEK! THE PEOPLE WHO STOLE HELEN WILL HEAR FROM US ALL.

BROTHER, WHAT'S YOUR PLAN?

AGAMEMNON LISTENED TO HIS AGGRIEVED BROTHER RAGE ON, BUT AS HE DID, HIS MIND FILLED WITH OTHER THOUGHTS. AGAMEMNON WOULD NOT LET THIS OPPORTUNITY PASS.

FIRST TO RECEIVE AGAMEMNON'S CALL WAS THE CUNNING AND COURAGEOUS ODYSSEUS, KING OF ITHACA, A MAN DEVOTED TO – ABOVE ALL THINGS – HIS KINGDOM AND FAMILY.

A MESSENGER FROM AGAMEMNON. WITH THAT WOMAN'S ABDUCTION, HE'S FINALLY FOUND HIS EXCUSE.

TELL THE MESSENGER WHEN HE ARRIVES THAT I'M PLOWING MY FIELDS.

YES, SIRE.

WHERE IS YOUR KING? I COME WITH A MESSAGE FOR HIM.

HE'S IN THE VALLEY, PLOWING HIS FIELDS,

PALAMEDES WENT TO CONVEY AGAMEMNON'S ORDERS TO THE NOTORIOUSLY WILY ODYSSEUS, DEMANDING HE JOIN THE COALITION. ODYSSEUS, THOUGH, IS NOT SO EAGER TO SUPPORT THE GREEDY KING'S VAINGLORIOUS ADVENTURE. INSTEAD, HE FEIGNS MADNESS, PLOWING HIS FIELDS WITH SALT.

AREN'T YOU ODYSSEUS'S WIFE? WHAT A LOVELY CHILD YOU HAVE THERE.

I'LL PUT HIS INFANT SON IN FRONT OF THE PLOW. LET'S SEE HOW FAR HE'LL TAKE THIS TRICK.

PALAMEDES, WELL AWARE OF ODYSSEUS' CUNNING NATURE, IMMEDIATELY SUSPECTS THE ITHACAN KING IS UP TO HIS USUAL GAMES...

FIRST THEY ENLISTED THE MASSIVE AND MIGHTY AJAX, FAMOUS FOR HIS HUGE SHIELD OF COWHIDE AND BRONZE.

NEXT, THE PAIR CONSCRIPTED DIOMEDES, THE YOUNGEST OF THE ACHAEAN KINGS. AFTER ACHILLES, HE WAS THE MOST SKILLED WARRIOR.

THEN ODYSSEUS AND PALAMEDES SOUGHT OUT NESTOR, THE OLDEST OF THE KINGS, WHO BROUGHT WISDOM AND PERSPECTIVE TO THE ALLIANCE.

PHILOCTETES WAS NEXT ON THEIR LIST. HIS MASSIVE BOW ONCE BELONGED TO HERAKLES HIMSELF.

ODYSSEUS AND PALAMEDES CARRIED ON UNTIL AT LAST THEY ARRIVED AT THE HOME OF PROTESILAUS, A SOLDIER FULL OF ENTHUSIASM AND NEWLY MARRIED.

WHY DO YOU HAVE TO GO? WE'VE JUST MARRIED.

DUTY.

SEE. HE UNDERSTANDS LOYALTY AND DUTY.

LET'S HOPE HE LIVES LONG ENOUGH TO UNDERSTAND THE DIFFERENCE.

DIFFERENCE?

I HAVE A DUTY TO MY WIFE AND FAMILY, BUT I'LL GIVE MY LOYALTY ONLY TO THOSE WHO DESERVE IT.

DON'T WORRY. OUR GOOD KING WILL HAVE HIS HANDS FULL WITH ACHILLES.

HA! DON'T LET AGAMEMNON HEAR THAT!

CHAPTER SIX

A WIND FROM THE WEST

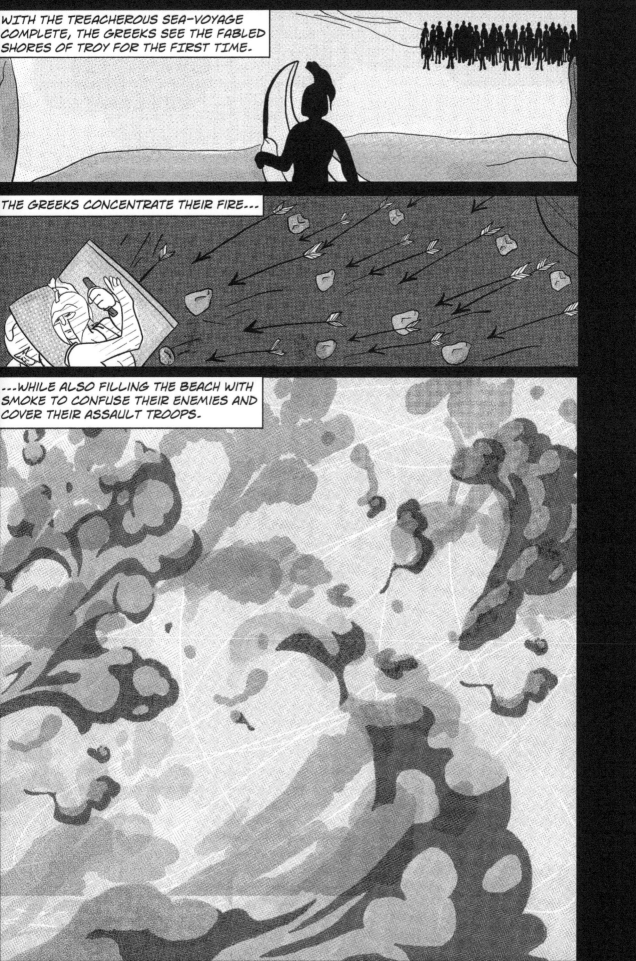

WITH THE TREACHEROUS SEA-VOYAGE COMPLETE, THE GREEKS SEE THE FABLED SHORES OF TROY FOR THE FIRST TIME.

THE GREEKS CONCENTRATE THEIR FIRE...

...WHILE ALSO FILLING THE BEACH WITH SMOKE TO CONFUSE THEIR ENEMIES AND COVER THEIR ASSAULT TROOPS.

ODYSSEUS WAS TRUE TO HIS WORD. HE SPRINGS FORWARD BOLDLY OFF THE SHIP, SEEMINGLY UNAFRAID OF THE PROPHECY.

PARTIALLY HIDDEN BY THE SMOKE AND FOG OF BATTLE, ODYSSEUS, *IT APPEARS*, HAS DEFIED THE PROPHECY AND BEEN THE FIRST TO SET FOOT ON TROJAN SOIL ... AND *LIVED!*

ON ME, BOYS! LET'S TAKE THIS BEACH.

I HAD TO BREAK THE CURSE... FOR THE GREATER GOOD...

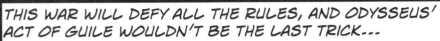

THIS WAR WILL DEFY ALL THE RULES, AND ODYSSEUS' ACT OF GUILE WOULDN'T BE THE LAST TRICK...

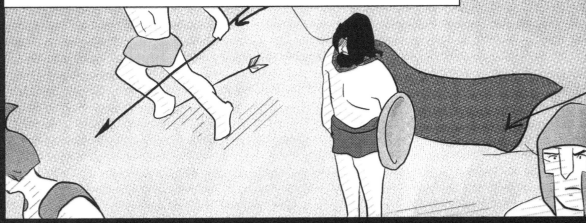

...NOR WOULD PROTESILAUS BE THE LAST INNOCENT TO DIE.

CHAPTER SEVEN

LET SLIP THE DOG OF WARS

WHEN THE GREEKS LAND AT TROY AND THE FIGHTING BEGINS, ZEUS REALIZES THAT THE WAR WILL COME HOME TO MT OLYMPUS. THE GODS ARE DIVIDED IN THEIR LOYALTIES AND OLD GRIEVANCES WILL BE FOUGHT OUT THROUGH MORTAL PROXIES.

YOU KILLED OUR PRIESTS!

YOU HELPED ABDUCT HELEN!

ZEUS, THE CLOUD-CRASHER, REFLECTS ON THE COMING YEARS OF SAVAGE FIGHTING, YEARNING FOR THE DAYS OF BANQUETING AND PLENTY. TOO LATE, THE SON OF CRONUS, REALIZED THAT WHEN MORTALS FIGHT, EVEN THE MIGHTY GODS SUFFER. FOR, IF THE GODS AREN'T WORSHIPPED, THEY CEASE TO EXIST.

91

ACHILLES TELLS PATROCLUS ABOUT A TIME WHEN HE WAS ON THE VERGE OF MANHOOD AND HIS MOTHER CONSULTED THE ORACLE AT DELPHI ABOUT HIS FUTURE.

WHAT DO YOU SEE?

GLORY... SORRY. A GREAT WAR WILL CONSUME A GENERATION OF HEROES. YOUR SON, ACHILLES, WILL BE CALLED TO THAT WAR. IF HE SEES THE WALLS OF TROY, HE **WILL** DIE AND...

WHAT ELSE?!

...HIS FAME WILL LIVE FOREVER. SO SAYETH THE ORACLE.

ON THE LONG WALK HOME FROM DELPHI, THETIS' MIND WAS TROUBLED. ACHILLES COULD FEEL HIS MOTHER'S CONCERN.

MOTHER, MY HEEL IS BLISTERED.

THEN LET'S SIT BY THE ROAD HERE AND REST OUR FEET AWHILE.

HE'S STILL A BOY. I'D DO ANYTHING TO KEEP HIM SAFE.

MOTHER, YOU HAVE TO TELL ME WHAT THE ORACLE SAID.

OF COURSE, TOMORROW WAS NOT ACHILLES' FATED DAY TO DIE, NOR FOR THE DAYS THAT FOLLOWED. LITTLE HAPPENED FOR THE NEXT WEEK— UNTIL TROY'S ALLIES BEGAN TO ARRIVE. FIRST THE ETHIOPIANS CAME TO SUPPORT THE BELEAGUERED CITY.

ACHILLES STRIDES OUT OF HIS TENT, RESPLENDENT IN HIS ARMOR. AS BATTLE LOOMS, HIS FOCUS SHARPENS TO A FINE EDGE.

AS DAWN BROKE, THE EARLY MORNING LIGHT FLASHED OFF THE WARRIORS' CRUEL BRAZEN WEAPONS AND THE GOLD ANKLET OF MEMNON, KING OF THE ETHIOPIANS.

FROM THE WALLS OF TROY, ACHILLES' "GLORY" TOOK ON A DIFFERENT PERSPECTIVE.

BACK IN HIS TENT, ACHILLES PRESENTS PATROCLUS WITH A GIFT—MEMNON'S GILDED ANKLET.

HORROR

WAR IS HATEFUL TO MOTHERS.

YOURS. NOW GIVE ME QUIET. I NEED WINE. LOTS OF IT.

DAY AFTER DAY, THE REMORSELESS SLAUGHTER CONTINUED, AND ACHILLES KILLED MEN INTO THE HUNDREDS.

NEXT, WHEN THE AMAZONS ARRIVED, THE ARMIES OF THE GREEKS WERE DRIVEN BACK BY THE FEROCIOUS TRIBE OF WARRIOR WOMEN. ONCE AGAIN, AGAMEMNON AND THE GREEK KINGS TURNED TO ACHILLES IN THEIR HOUR OF NEED. THE GREEK WARRIOR WOULD HAVE TO FIGHT, YET AGAIN.

AMIDST THE SLAUGHTER, PENTHESILEA, QUEEN OF THE AMAZONS, AND ACHILLES FOUND EACH OTHER ON THE BLOOD-SOAKED BATTLEFIELD. BEAUTIFUL IN HER LETHALITY, HER APPEARANCE DISTRACTS ACHILLES FROM THE TASKS AT HAND.

FOCUS... GET HER OUT OF YOUR HEAD!

OH SUCH A PRETTY ONE! HE'LL MAKE A FINE TROPHY ON MY WALL.

RAIN SMOOTHS PENTHESILEA'S LUSTROUS HAIR. THEIR BLOOD FLOWS IN RIVULETS BENEATH THE LETHAL BLOWS. THOSE AROUND THEM, MYRMIDONS AND AMAZONS ALIKE, ARE CAPTIVATED BY THE FATAL DANCE.

WHO IS THIS MAN? I'VE NEVER FOUGHT A MAN LIKE HIM.... HE DOESN'T TIRE, HE DOESN'T STOP, HE'S LIKE A GOD.

FEINT LEFT—STRIKE RIGHT.

ACHILLES SEES HIS OPENING. HE IMPALES THE GREAT QUEEN WITH BLINDING SPEED.

SUCH BEAUTY, SUCH LOVELY HAIR.

ACHILLES TOOK HIS WORTHY OPPONENT'S BODY TO HONOR HER WITH A WARRIOR'S FUNERAL.

DEATH IS BEAUTIFUL....

WHAT CAN I DO FOR YOU?

KEEP THIS. IT'S THE QUEEN'S HAIR CLASP. I WANT YOU TO WEAR IT. I WANT YOU TO REMIND ME OF HER.

FOLLOWING THE CUSTOMS OF THE DAY, ACHILLES CONDUCTED THE CUSTOMARY FUNERAL RITES FOR HIS WORTHY ADVERSARY.

WHAT'S WRONG? YOU'VE KILLED BEFORE?

I DON'T KNOW. SOMETHING'S DIFFERENT.

THE KILLING AND DYING CONTINUED. THERE WAS NO END IN SIGHT. ACHILLES FOUGHT ON NOT KNOWING WHEN HIS DAY WOULD COME BUT KNOWING THAT IT **WOULD** COME.

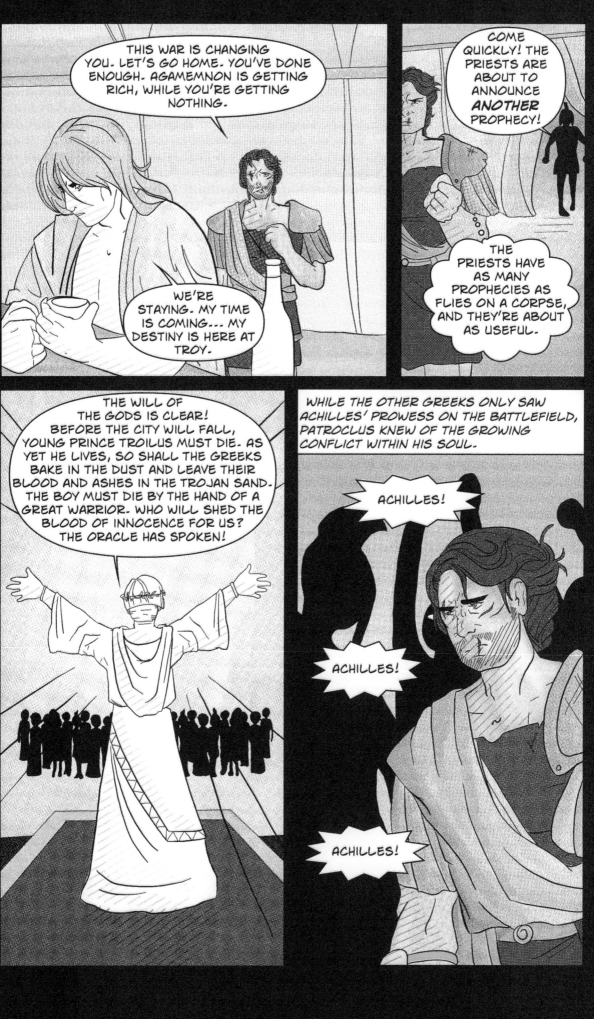

CHAPTER EIGHT

STALEMATE

HOPES ARE REVIVED AS THE PROUD AMAZONS WALK THROUGH THE CROWD. THE TROJANS HAD NEVER SEEN AN ARMY LIKE THIS... AN ARMY OF WOMEN.

THEY'RE MAGNIFICENT!

THEY'RE TERRIFYING!

MOMMY, WHY DO THEY HAVE THOSE SCARS?

CAPTAIN MYRINA OF THE AMAZONS STOPS TO ANSWER THE CHILD'S QUESTION AS HER SISTER-WARRIORS MARCH ON.

THE BETTER TO DRAW THE BOW STRING!

HOPES THAT RAN HIGH IN THE MORNING WERE DASHED ON THE ROCK OF DESPAIR IN THE EVENING. THE AMAZONS RETURNED WITHOUT THE BODY OF THEIR BELOVED QUEEN.

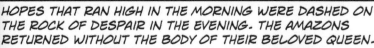

THEY SAY HE KEPT THE QUEEN'S BODY.

THEY SAY HE FELL IN LOVE WITH HER... WITH HER CORPSE.

WHAT WAS LEFT OF THE AMAZON ARMY MARCHED TOWARD THEIR BARRACKS IN THE EAST OF TROY.

HELEN VISITS THE WOUNDED AMAZONS.

YOU'RE WOUNDED...

I SEE YOU'RE NOT.

SHE'S RIGHT!

WHEN LITTLE TROILUS'S HEADLESS BODY IS RETURNED TO THE PALACE, THE FIGHTING TAKES ON A NEW INTENSITY.

IF ACHILLES IS CAPABLE OF THIS, WE'RE IN TROUBLE.

THIS ISN'T WAR—THIS IS MURDER

PARIS, WE DID THIS. WHAT ARE YOU GOING TO DO ABOUT IT?

WILL I HAVE TO FACE THIS MAN?

HECTOR AND DEIPHOBUS CONTINUE TO WREAK HAVOC AMONGST THE GREEKS.

AJAX, MENELAUS, ODYSSEUS, AND THE OTHER GREEKS MAKE MANY WIDOWS AMONG THE TROJANS.

IN A WAR LIKE THIS, ONLY THE JACKALS AND RAVENS PROSPER. WHEN MORTALS ARE OCCUPIED BY BURNING THE FALLEN ON PYRES, THE GODS ARE DENIED THE SWEET SMOKE OF SACRIFICIAL OFFERINGS.

AS ZEUS' EAGLE SURVEYS THE RAVAGED BATTLEFIELD FROM ON HIGH, IT SEES THE CIRCUMSTANCES OF ALL INVOLVED.

MANY OF THE HEROES WERE FAVORED BY THE GODS. ATHENA FAVORED DIOMEDES, ENCOURAGING AND PROTECTING HIM IN BATTLE AS MUCH AS SHE WAS ABLE.

WHEREVER THE TROJAN PRINCE AENEAS FOUGHT, HIS MOTHER AND PROTECTRESS, APHRODITE, WAS NEVER FAR. THE TWO RIVAL GODDESSES USED THEIR MORTAL HEROES TO SETTLE THEIR HEAVENLY DISPUTES.

FATE BROUGHT AENEAS AND DIOMEDES FATE-TO-FACE ON THE BATTLEFIELD. AS THE TWO HEROES PREPARED TO DUEL, EACH SUPPORTED BY THEIR PATRON GODDESS, THE FIGHTING CEASED AROUND THEM.

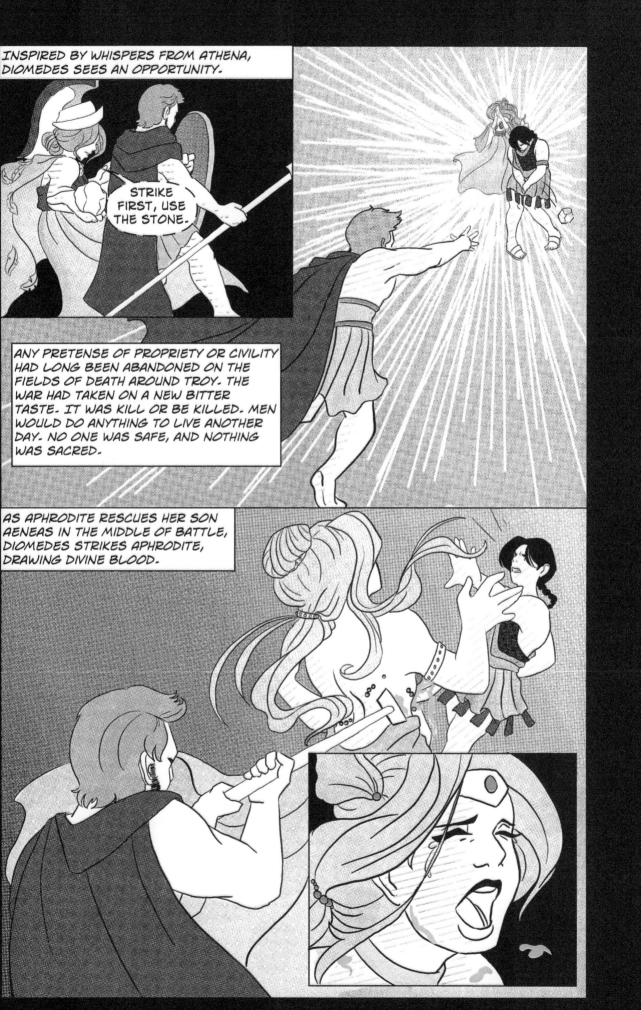

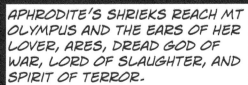

APHRODITE'S SHRIEKS REACH MT OLYMPUS AND THE EARS OF HER LOVER, ARES, DREAD GOD OF WAR, LORD OF SLAUGHTER, AND SPIRIT OF TERROR.

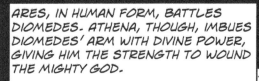

ARES, IN HUMAN FORM, BATTLES DIOMEDES. ATHENA, THOUGH, IMBUES DIOMEDES' ARM WITH DIVINE POWER, GIVING HIM THE STRENGTH TO WOUND THE MIGHTY GOD.

DIOMEDES— YOU'RE MINE!

THE WOUNDED GODS DEPART, AND AN EERIE CALM SETTLES OVER THE BATTLEFIELD.

THIS WAR IS TEARING THE WORLD APART.

WHAT WILL STOP THIS WAR?

ONLY SOMETHING TERRIBLE!

WHEN WILL THIS WAR END?

CHAPTER NINE

LIVE AND LET LIVE

119

THE NEXT DAY, BOTH SIDES SEND PARTIES AMONG THE FALLEN TO CLAIM THEIR DEAD.

THE GREEKS ARE DISTURBED BY WHAT THEY SEE...

THIS WAR IS BLEEDING GREECE DRY.

...AS ARE THE TROJANS.

CAN THIS BE? SO MANY DEAD. I KNEW THESE MEN...

LEADERS OF BOTH SIDES WANDER AND SOON FIND THEMSELVES WITHIN SIGHT OF EACH OTHER.

I HOPE THESE KINGS KNOW WHAT THEY'RE DOING.

THAT'D BE A FIRST!

KEEP YOUR SWORDS HANDY. THESE GREEKS ARE TRICKY.

WHAT IS THAT DEVIOUS GREEK UP TO?

WHY DO YOU HESITATE, BROTHER? SURELY ANY TROJAN CAN BEST ANY OF THE LONG-HAIRED GREEKS.

I EXPECTED MORE FROM SOMEONE WHO CALLS HIMSELF MAN-SLAYER. DOES THE IDEA FRIGHTEN YOU? OR, PERHAPS YOU DON'T HAVE THE AUTHORITY TO SPEAK FOR THE TROJANS. SEND ME YOUR FATHER TO DISCUSS THESE MATTERS... OR YOUR MOTHER. I HEAR SHE'S THE REAL POWER BEHIND THE THRONE.

WATCH YOUR TONGUE, FAT KING. YOU LOOK LIKE YOU HAVEN'T SWUNG A SWORD FOR A WHILE. I SPEAK FOR TROY AND HER ARMIES.

THEN SPEAK!

SEIZING HIS MOMENT, ODYSSEUS PUTS HIS PLAN INTO MOTION.
DO YOU AGREE? CHAMPIONS?
THE GREEKS AGREE! TRIAL BY CHAMPIONS!
AS DOES TROY! WE'LL DO IT THE OLD WAY.
ACHILLES WILL STAND FOR THE GREEKS.
AND I WILL MEET HIM FOR TROY.
KISS YOUR WIFE AND CHILD TONIGHT, HECTOR. TOMORROW, YOU BURN ON A FUNERAL PYRE.
I BEG YOUR PARDON, GOOD LORDS, BUT THIS WAR BEGAN WITH THE SLIGHT OF ONE MAN AGAINST ANOTHER. WHILE THE FIGHT BETWEEN GODDESS-BORN ACHILLES AND HECTOR THE GREAT HORSE-TAMER WOULD BE A SIGHT TO BEHOLD, WOULDN'T IT BE MORE APPROPRIATE IF THIS CONFLICT WAS SETTLED BY THE ORIGINAL BELLIGERENTS? SURELY SUCH A CONTEST WOULD BE BOTH JUST AND PLEASING TO THE GODS.

HECTOR EXPLAINS THE VOW HE HAS MADE THAT PARIS WILL FIGHT A DUEL AGAINST THE GREEK CHAMPION ACHILLES.

THE FATE OF EVERY MAN, WOMAN, AND CHILD RESTS WITH PARIS.

OATHS HAVE BEEN MADE TO THE GODS.

IS HE READY?

I'VE TRAINED HIM WELL. I'VE SENT A THOUSAND MEN TO HADES WITH MY SPEAR. I COULD KILL A THOUSAND MORE AND NOTHING WOULD CHANGE. HE CAN END THIS WAR BY KILLING JUST ONE. WE HAVE TO TRY.

PARIS STILL FIGHTS FOR THIS WOMAN— NOT FOR THE CITY.

REMEMBER THAT NIGHT IN SPARTA? YOU HELPED START THIS WAR. NOW, BE BRAVE ENOUGH TO HELP END IT. LOOK AT YOUR BROTHERS— LOOK AT WHAT THEY'VE DONE. BE A PRINCE OF TROY. FIGHT MENELAUS. IF YOU DON'T, YOU'LL NEVER TOUCH ME AGAIN.

YES... YES, YOU'RE RIGHT. NOW IT'S MY TURN.

WORD OF THE IMPENDING DUEL SPREADS THROUGHOUT THE GREEK CAMP AS PATROCLUS BRINGS WORD OF IT TO ACHILLES.

GO SEE THAT BRUTE MENELAUS HACK THE BOY TO DEATH IF YOU WANT. I'VE SEEN ENOUGH DEATH. THIS WAR WILL NEVER LEAVE ME.

MENELAUS WILL MAKE SHORT WORK OF PARIS. SOON THIS WAR WILL BE OVER, AND WE CAN GO HOME TOGETHER.

THE MEN WILL EXPECT TO SEE YOU THERE, ACHILLES.

I SAID NO! YOU BE ACHILLES IF YOU THINK YOU'RE UP FOR IT. THE ACHILLES THEY KNOW IS JUST A MYTH ANYWAY.

THE CHAMPIONS CLASH AGAIN AND AGAIN. THE FIGHT GOES ON LONGER THAN ANYONE EXPECTED.

END THIS, BROTHER! BE DONE WITH HIM!

PARIS CONTINUES TO TAUNT THE LARGER WARRIOR, BUT MENELAUS NO LONGER PAYS ANY ATTENTION, FALLING INTO A COLD, CALCULATING ANGER.

MENELAUS STRIKES, AND THE YOUNG PRINCE BARELY AVOIDS THE BLOW. MENELAUS COMES AT PARIS AGAIN RELENTLESSLY.

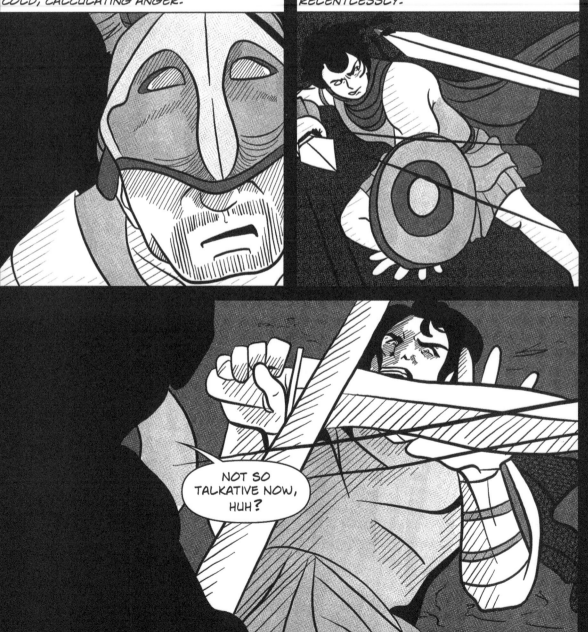

NOT SO TALKATIVE NOW, HUH?

AS HELEN BEGINS HER TRAINING WITH THE AMAZONS...

HA! YOU THINK YOU'RE UP FOR IT, PRINCESS? ALL THAT BLOOD, GUTS, AND SCREAMING?

I'M NO PRINCESS— YOU AMAZONS ARE FURIES!

DAMN RIGHT! FURIES FROM HELL!

IT SOON BECOMES APPARENT...

THERE IS MORE TO HER THAN JEWELS AND GRACE.

ALL THE WHILE, THE GREEKS AND TROJANS ARE DESPERATE FOR VICTORY.

THE FIGHTING REACHES A FEVERISH PITCH.

THE GREEKS SUFFER GREAT LOSSES BUT INFLICT JUST AS MANY AS WELL.

EVEN SACRED PRIESTS AND PRIESTESSES— ONCE RESPECTED BY ALL— ARE CAPTURED AND SOLD INTO SLAVERY. THE OLD RULES GOVERNING WARFARE SLIP AWAY AS BOTH SIDES SLIDE FURTHER INTO BARBARITY.

AGAMEMNON EXERTS HIS AUTHORITY AND CLAIMS THE BEST PRIZES FOR HIMSELF AMONGST THE CAPTIVES, INCLUDING THE PRIESTESS OF APOLLO, BRISEIS.

I'LL TAKE HER!

BUT SHE WAS CAPTURED BY ACHILLES' MEN.

I DON'T CARE. CLEAN HER UP, AND TAKE HER TO MY TENT.

CHAPTER TEN

WHERE'S HIS BEAUTIFUL HEAD?

THE MYRMIDONS TEAR INTO THE TROJANS WITH FRIGHTENING EASE. THE TROJAN ATTACK QUICKLY STALLS.

PATROCLUS, MORE THAN ANY OTHER GREEK WARRIOR, LEAVES BODIES IN HIS WAKE.

HECTOR, NEARBY, STILL MANAGES TO CLAIM MANY GREEK LIVES.

THE FIGHTING SHIFTS IN THE GREEKS' FAVOR. HECTOR ORDERS HIS SOLDIERS TO FALL BACK BEFORE THEY ARE COMPLETELY ROUTED.

PATROCLUS SPIES HECTOR THROUGH THE CHAOS.

HECTOR, STAND AND FIGHT, YOU COWARD!

139

EVEN ABOVE THE DIN OF BATTLE, HECTOR HEARS THE CHALLENGE, WHICH HE ASSUMES COMES FROM THE MIGHTY ACHILLES. HOWEVER, HE IS MORE CONCERNED WITH PRESERVING HIS ARMY. SO, HE ORDERS HIS TROOPS TO PULL BACK TO THE SAFETY OF TROY'S WALLS.

BACK, MEN!

I WANT THAT MAN'S HEAD, BUT I PROMISED ACHILLES I WOULD NOT PURSUE HIM TO THE GATES....

WHAT DO YOU WANT, ODYSSEUS?

I KNOW WHO YOU ARE—PATROCLUS. THE REAL ACHILLES WOULD NEVER STOP. THIS IS YOUR MOMENT. KILL HECTOR. GO! HURRY, BEFORE HE REACHES SAFETY!

PATROCLUS' BLOOD IS UP. HE FORGETS HIS PROMISE TO ACHILLES AND GIVES CHASE TO HECTOR.

HECTOR, YOU COWARDLY DOG! ARE YOU RUNNING AWAY IN FRONT OF YOUR SON? IN FRONT OF YOUR WIFE? IN FRONT OF YOUR FATHER? IN FRONT OF THE GODS?!

FIGHT ME!

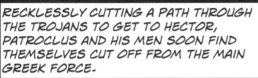
RECKLESSLY CUTTING A PATH THROUGH THE TROJANS TO GET TO HECTOR, PATROCLUS AND HIS MEN SOON FIND THEMSELVES CUT OFF FROM THE MAIN GREEK FORCE.

WELL, MIGHTY ACHILLES, YOU AND YOUR MEN ARE SURROUNDED.

I'M GOING TO FEED YOUR GUTS TO THE DOGS. I'M GOING TO EAT YOUR HEART.

NOW THAT WE'RE FACE TO FACE, YOU LOOK JUST LIKE ANY OTHER MAN I'VE KILLED.

HECTOR ORDERS HIS MEN NOT TO INTERFERE. PATROCLUS, IN HIS GUISE AS ACHILLES, DOES LIKEWISE.

HECTOR, YOUR WIFE WILL BE A WIDOW BY SUNDOWN. I HEAR SHE'S A REAL BEAUTY. PITY SHE AND YOUR SON HAVE TO DIE.

YOU TALK A LOT— LET'S GET THIS ON.

THE TWO HEROES FIGHT WITH BLINDING SPEED. EVERYONE WHO WATCHES IS STRUCK WITH AWE. NEITHER MAN SEEMS ABLE TO BEST THE OTHER— BUT THEN...

HECTOR– THE REAPER OF MEN– FINDS AN OPENING AND STRIKES, DEALING WHAT HE BELIEVES TO BE A MORTAL BLOW TO THE GREAT ACHILLES.

DIE!

AHAHAH–

ACHILLES, I'M SORRY.

THE SOLDIERS OF TROY ARE OVERJOYED, BELIEVING ACHILLES TO BE DEAD. THE MYRMIDONS CAN NOT BELIEVE WHAT THEY'VE JUST SEEN.

THIS CAN'T BE...

LORD ACHILLES– NO!

NO!!!!!

BUT A GLINT FROM THE ARMOR CATCHES HECTOR'S ATTENTION. HE BENDS DOWN TO SEE A LOCKET OF HAIR WRAPPED IN GOLD HANGING AROUND THE DEAD MAN'S NECK AND SUDDENLY REALIZES HIS MISTAKE.

THIS BELONGED TO PENTHESILEA! ACHILLES KEPT IT AS A TROPHY AND GAVE IT TO PATROCLUS. ACHILLES IS STILL ALIVE, AND I MUST FACE HIM.

HECTOR ORDERS HIS MEN TO KILL THE REMAINING MYRMIDONS AND STRIP PATROCLUS OF ACHILLES' ARMOR.

PUT THEIR HEADS ON PIKES. LEAVE THE BODIES FOR THE BIRDS.

THE AMAZONS WILL WANT BACK THE LAST REMAINS OF THEIR QUEEN.

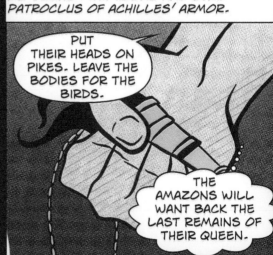

THE GREEKS ARE AFRAID TO ANSWER.
ACHILLES IS A DANGER TO **EVERYONE**

WHERE'S PATROCLUS' HEAD?

WHERE'S HIS HEAD?!

WHERE'S HIS BEAUTIFUL HEAD!!!

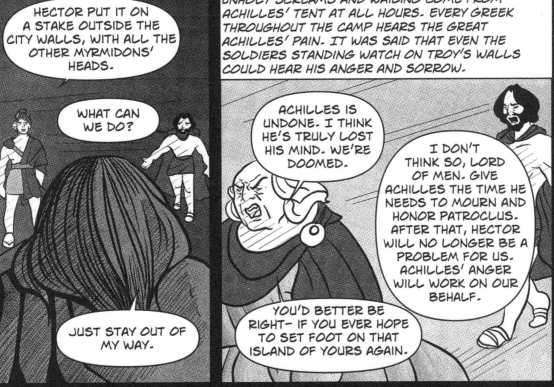

HECTOR PUT IT ON A STAKE OUTSIDE THE CITY WALLS, WITH ALL THE OTHER MYRMIDONS' HEADS.

WHAT CAN WE DO?

JUST STAY OUT OF MY WAY.

UNHOLY SCREAMS AND WAILING COME FROM ACHILLES' TENT AT ALL HOURS. EVERY GREEK THROUGHOUT THE CAMP HEARS THE GREAT ACHILLES' PAIN. IT WAS SAID THAT EVEN THE SOLDIERS STANDING WATCH ON TROY'S WALLS COULD HEAR HIS ANGER AND SORROW.

ACHILLES IS UNDONE. I THINK HE'S TRULY LOST HIS MIND. WE'RE DOOMED.

I DON'T THINK SO, LORD OF MEN. GIVE ACHILLES THE TIME HE NEEDS TO MOURN AND HONOR PATROCLUS. AFTER THAT, HECTOR WILL NO LONGER BE A PROBLEM FOR US. ACHILLES' ANGER WILL WORK ON OUR BEHALF.

YOU'D BETTER BE RIGHT— IF YOU EVER HOPE TO SET FOOT ON THAT ISLAND OF YOURS AGAIN.

WHILE ACHILLES THUNDERED AND STORMED, ODYSSEUS USED THE TIME TO CONSIDER THE GREEKS' NEXT MOVE.

RAGE ON, NOBLE ACHILLES. RAGE AGAINST THE GODS THEMSELVES. TURN YOUR ANGER TO HECTOR. WE'LL USE YOUR PAIN TO END THIS WAR.

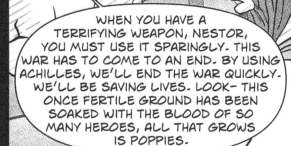

ACHILLES IS A DANGEROUS MAN, ODYSSEUS. HE'S AS DANGEROUS TO THEM AS HE IS TO US.

WHEN YOU HAVE A TERRIFYING WEAPON, NESTOR, YOU MUST USE IT SPARINGLY. THIS WAR HAS TO COME TO AN END. BY USING ACHILLES, WE'LL END THE WAR QUICKLY. WE'LL BE SAVING LIVES. LOOK- THIS ONCE FERTILE GROUND HAS BEEN SOAKED WITH THE BLOOD OF SO MANY HEROES, ALL THAT GROWS IS POPPIES.

WAR... IT OPENS PANDORA'S BOX OF EVIL.

INSPIRATION SUDDENLY COMES TO ODYSSEUS, AS IF WHISPERED TO HIM BY ATHENA HERSELF.

COME, NESTOR, WE'LL NEED A FEW MEN.

THE KING OF ITHACA SEEKS OUT THE MOST SKILLED BLACKSMITH WHO TRAVELED TO TROY WITH THE GREEK ARMY.

HEPHAESTUS!

YES, MY LORD?

ODYSSEUS EXPLAINS WHAT HE WANTS TO THE ARMORER.

WHAT IS IT? I'VE NEVER SEEN ORE LIKE THAT.

THEY CALL IT IRON. KEEP THIS A GREAT SECRET— IT WILL CHANGE WAR FOREVER.

MAKE ME A SWORD. IT'LL TAKE THE HEAT OF THE SUN TO FORGE IT. THIS MUST BE THE BEST WORK! I NEED IT DONE NOW. NESTOR AND MY MEN WILL GET YOU ANYTHING YOU NEED.

IT MIGHT BE POSSIBLE TO GIVE YOU WHAT YOU WANT, BUT WE'VE STRIPPED THE NEARBY LAND OF MOST OF ITS RESOURCES. I HAVE TO TRAVEL OVER A DAY NOW JUST TO FIND FUEL FOR THE FORGES.

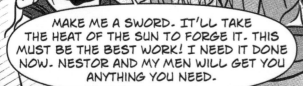

USE THE SHIPS TO FUEL YOUR FORGE. WITH HALF OUR ARMY LYING DEAD IN THE FIELDS, WE NEED FEWER SHIPS TO GET HOME. GET IT DONE.

YES, MY LORD.

HEPHAESTUS WORKS, PAUSING FOR SHORT MOMENTS TO EAT OR DRINK.

AS THE MASTER OF THE FORGE WORKS AWAY, ATHENA, IN DISGUISE, WALKS AMONGST THE GREEK CAMP.

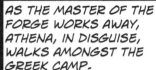

AT THE END OF TWO DAYS NON-STOP WORK, HEPHAESTUS FINISHES HIS TASK.

THEY'VE DISCOVERED IRON! NOW THIS RACE OF MEN TRULY HAS THE POWER TO DESTROY THEMSELVES! THEY'LL USE THIS TO DESTROY THE GODS— THEY'LL BECOME DESTROYER OF WORLDS.

HEPHAESTUS, YOU'VE OUTDONE YOURSELF.

THANKS, MY LORDS.

WHAT HAVE I DONE? I'VE BUILT A WEAPON LIKE NO OTHER— IT'S TOO POWERFUL.

IT'S A WEAPON, LIKE NO OTHER. USE IT TO—

KILL HECTOR!

DON'T WORRY, I KNOW WHAT YOU WANT ME TO DO. PATROCLUS TOLD ME. HE'S DEAD. HE KNOWS EVERYTHING NOW. OH?! WHAT'S THAT YOU HAVE?

ODYSSEUS WALKS PAST THE RIVER ON HIS RETURN TO HIS TENT. HE SEES FIRSTHAND WHAT ACHILLES MEANT BY "PRACTICE".

THE TROJAN PRISONERS! HE'S KILLED THEM ALL.

EVEN APHRODITE AND CUPID WEEP AT THE GRIEF OF ACHILLES. POPPIES SOON GROW WHERE THE GODDESS' TEARS MIX WITH PATROCLUS' BLOOD IN THE RED DUST WHERE HE DIED.

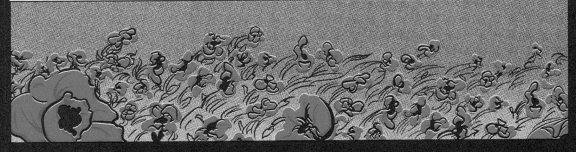

151

HECTOR DRINKS IN THE MEMORY OF HIS WIFE AND SON BEFORE PREPARING TO FACE ACHILLES. HE STRUGGLES TO SAY GOOD-BYE. THE FINALITY OF SUCH WORDS IS DIFFICULT FOR HIM TO BEAR. AT THE SAME TIME, ANDROMACHE STEELS HERSELF FOR WHAT IS TO COME.

CHAPTER ELEVEN

PAWNS IN A GAME

ACHILLES IS JUST STANDING THERE. HE WON'T LEAVE UNTIL HE FIGHTS HECTOR.

SPEAK, MESSENGER.

HE'S NOT THE ONLY ONE WHO LOST SOMEONE HE LOVES, AFTER ALL.

IT'S PRINCE HECTOR, SIRE. HE'S ON HIS WAY TO MEET ACHILLES. HE WON'T BE TALKED OUT OF IT.

STOP THE PRINCE! ORDER THE GUARDS TO HOLD HIM!

AT THE MAIN GATES OF THE CITY, THE GUARDS REFUSE TO ALLOW PRINCE HECTOR TO LEAVE. THE KING AND QUEEN SOON CATCH UP WITH HIM.

WHY DO YOU THINK YOU MUST DO THIS, SON?

YOU SAID IT YOURSELF— THE GREEKS AREN'T TRUSTWORTHY OR HONORABLE.

SHORTLY, PARIS, HELEN, AND ANDROMACHE ARRIVE.

WHAT'S THIS I HEAR? YOU'RE GOING TO FIGHT THAT SAVAGE?

ACHILLES IS A BRUTISH KILLER... YEARNS FOR DEATH... PLEASE DON'T... NOT ON MY ACCOUNT.

155

THE TWO HEROES SIZE ONE ANOTHER UP.

HECTOR, YOU OLD WOMAN, ARE YOU FINISHED SHAKING BEHIND YOUR WALLS?

PATROCLUS WAS A WORTHY OPPONENT. YOU CAN BE PROUD OF HOW HE FOUGHT. I RESPECTED HIM AND FEEL YOUR LOSS. WOULD HE BE PROUD OF YOU NOW? PEACE COULD START HERE— WITH US.

PEACE? I SPIT ON YOUR PEACE! PEACE IS FOR THE WEAK. I'LL GIVE YOU PEACE— THE PEACE OF THE GRAVE.

SO BE IT.

ACHILLES, LET US MAKE A PACT BEFORE THE GODS THAT WHOEVER FALLS TODAY WILL BE GRANTED ALL THE PROPER FUNERAL RIGHTS BY THE VICTOR.

NEVER! DOGS AND VULTURES WILL FEAST ON YOUR FLESH! I'M GOING TO EAT YOUR HEART!

ALMIGHTY GODS, GIVE ME THE COURAGE AND STRENGTH TO FACE MY DEATH.

HECTOR STRIKES FIRST, BUT ACHILLES EASILY BLOCKS THE BLOW. GOD-LIKE ACHILLES HURLS HIS OWN SPEAR IN RETURN, WHICH MAN-KILLING HECTOR DODGES.

AS THE SHADOW OF DEATH
LENGTHENS OVER HECTOR, AND HE
SEES THE EDGE OF THE ABYSS, HIS
LAST THOUGHTS TURN TO HIS WIFE
AND SON. NEVER HAD HECTOR FELT
THE MAGNIFICENT BEAUTY OF LIFE
SO KEENLY.

DEATH IS NEAR.... WIFE, SON, I LOVE YOU.

THE FIGHT CONTINUES. BOTH MEN MOVE FAST. THE
CROWDS ON THE WALLS ABOVE, INCLUDING THE
ROYAL FAMILY, HAVE TROUBLE TELLING THE TWO
MEN APART. ACHILLES AND HECTOR FIGHT FOR
HOURS.

SEEMINGLY, HECTOR GAINS THE UPPER HAND,
KNOCKING ACHILLES' SWORD FROM HIS GRASP.

HECTOR'S FAMILY AND
ALL OF TROY REJOICE!

YES!

END THIS,
HECTOR!

YOU'VE
GOT HIM!

ACHILLES LOOKS FOR THE LOCKET OF PENTHESILEA'S HAIR HECTOR TOOK WHEN HE KILLED PATROCLUS.

WHERE IS IT? PATROCLUS WANTS HIS PRESENT BACK.

THE LOCKET IS NOWHERE TO BE FOUND. RAGE CONSUMES ACHILLES.

IF I CAN'T FIND PATROCLUS' PRESENT, I'LL GIVE HIM HECTOR AS A GIFT!

PIERCING HECTOR'S FEET FROM BEHIND HIS ANKLES, ACHILLES TIES THE PRINCE'S DEAD BODY TO HIS CHARIOT.

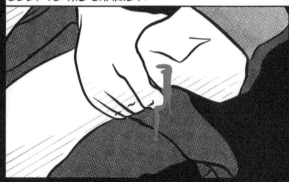

MOCKING THE TROJANS' GRIEF, MOCKING THE LAWS OF WAR, MOCKING EVERYTHING HUMAN, ACHILLES HEADS BACK TO CAMP. HE ALONE SEES THIS AS A TRIUMPH. TROJANS, GREEKS, AND EVEN THE GODS ARE UNITED IN THEIR DISGUST AT HIS CRIME.

ACHILLES LOOKS TO PRIAM AND SILENTLY POINTS TO HECTOR'S BODY.

AT LEAST THERE IS SOME HONOR LEFT AMONG THESE GREEKS.

REASON AT LAST. PRIAM, YOU'RE BRAVE FOR AN OLD MAN. WAR HAS MADE US ALL MAD. TAKE HECTOR'S BODY QUICKLY BEFORE ACHILLES CHANGES HIS MIND. I'LL LEAD YOU BACK TO TROY.

I CAN FIND MY WAY BACK ON MY OWN.

THE NEXT DAY, HECTOR'S FAMILY AND THE CITIZENS OF TROY GATHER BY THE GREAT HORSE ALTAR OF POSEIDON FOR THE LARGEST FUNERAL THE CITY HAS EVER SEEN, WITH DAYS OF GAMES, SACRIFICES TO THE GODS, AND FEASTS TO HONOR THE FALLEN PRINCE. AFTER NEARLY TEN YEARS OF SIEGE, YEARS THAT HAVE TAKEN A TOLL ON THE CITY, SCARCELY ENOUGH FOOD REMAINS TO FEED ALL THE MOURNERS. NEARING STARVATION, THE TROJANS HAVE EVEN RESORTED TO EATING THE LAST OF THEIR PRIZED HORSES.

HELEN'S LETTER INVITES ACHILLES TO A RENDEZVOUS WHERE SHE PROMISES TO GIVE HIM BACK PATROCLUS' LOCKET.

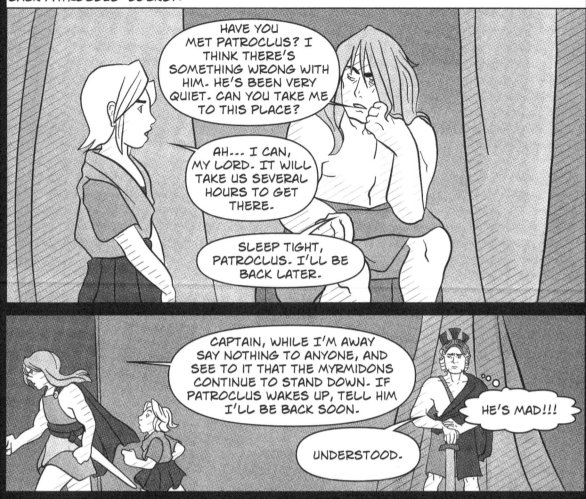

HAVE YOU MET PATROCLUS? I THINK THERE'S SOMETHING WRONG WITH HIM. HE'S BEEN VERY QUIET. CAN YOU TAKE ME TO THIS PLACE?

AH... I CAN, MY LORD. IT WILL TAKE US SEVERAL HOURS TO GET THERE.

SLEEP TIGHT, PATROCLUS. I'LL BE BACK LATER.

CAPTAIN, WHILE I'M AWAY SAY NOTHING TO ANYONE, AND SEE TO IT THAT THE MYRMIDONS CONTINUE TO STAND DOWN. IF PATROCLUS WAKES UP, TELL HIM I'LL BE BACK SOON.

HE'S MAD!!!

UNDERSTOOD.

EVEN IN HIS MADNESS, ACHILLES' INSTINCTS REMAIN SHARP. HOWEVER, HE IS CONSUMED WITH NOTHING BUT HATE AND RAGE. KNEELING NEXT TO THE YOUNG MESSENGER, HE KNOWS THE LAD HAS LED HIM TO HIS DESTINY AT LAST, AND HE SMILES THINLY.

LADY HELEN TOLD ME THIS IS AS FAR AS I AM TO GO, LORD ACHILLES. UP AHEAD IS A CLEARING, WHERE THE LADY IS WAITING FOR YOU.

RUN ALONG, LITTLE TROJAN PUP. I KNOW EXACTLY WHAT YOU'VE DONE, AND YOU'VE DONE IT WELL.

YOU'RE NOT GOING TO KILL ME?

NOT THIS TIME, BUT PRAY I NEVER SEE YOU AGAIN.

AMAZONS, GATHER OUR DEAD. LET THIS CARCASS ROT.

AS ZEUS STARES DOWN FROM ON HIGH, HE SURVEYS A PITIABLE SCENE. THE ONCE MIGHTY ACHILLES HAS BEEN REDUCED TO AN ALMOST UNRECOGNIZABLE PILE OF GORE. HOW THE MIGHTY HAVE FALLEN. GREAT ACHILLES, LIES DEAD, A VICTIM OF HIS OWN RAGE AND ANGER.

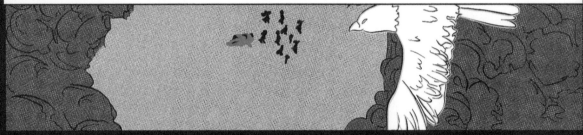

WHEN NIGHT FALLS, AND ACHILLES FAILS TO RETURN, CAPTAIN NEOPTOLEMUS GROWS CONCERNED.

YOU, SOLDIER, HAVE YOU SEEN OUR LORD?

THE CAPTAIN OF THE MYRMIDONS SEARCHES THE CAMP, BUT NO ONE HAS SEEN ACHILLES. WORRIED AND NOT KNOWING WHAT HAPPENED, NEOPTOLEMUS SEEKS ODYSSEUS' COUNSEL.

HE LEFT WITH A CHILD YOU SAY, AND YOU DON'T KNOW WHY?

YES, MY LORD.

ACHILLES IS THE STRONGEST AMONG US. I'M SURE HE CAN TAKE CARE OF HIMSELF, BUT WE'LL SEND OUT SEARCH PARTIES COME FIRST LIGHT.

AS ACHILLES' BODY MADE ITS WAY THROUGH THE GREEK CAMP IN A SOMBER PROCESSION, SOLDIERS CAME TO PAY THEIR RESPECTS TO THE SEEMINGLY INVINCIBLE WARRIOR. SUDDENLY, A GUST OF WIND BLEW BACK THE CORNER OF THE COVERING, AND THE MEN BEHELD ACHILLES' WOUNDED HEEL. FROM THAT MOMENT ON, A LEGEND GREW, A LEGEND OF A GREAT WARRIOR WITH ONLY ONE VULNERABILITY. BUT, THOSE WHO KNEW HIM WELL KNEW THE TRUTH: ACHILLES DIED THE MOMENT HECTOR KILLED PATROCLUS. THE AMAZONS HAD MERELY PUT HIM OUT OF HIS MISERY.

I THOUGHT NOTHING COULD TOUCH HIM.

HE'S DEAD? HOW COULD THIS HAPPEN?

LOOK, IT'S THE HEEL! THAT'S WHERE THEY GOT HIM!

ODYSSEUS INFORMS AGAMEMNON AND THE OTHER GREEK LORDS OF ACHILLES' FATE.

WHAT DO YOU MEAN THERE'S NOTHING LEFT? WHAT ARE WE TO CREMATE?

THE ARMY'S ON THE VERGE OF BREAKING. WE NEED A FUNERAL. WITHOUT IT, THE MEN WILL MUTINY.

THERE'S NO SHORTAGE OF BODIES TO BURN, LORD AGAMEMNON. YOU'VE MADE SURE OF THAT.

WATCH YOUR TONGUE, OR YOU'LL BE NEXT ON THE PYRE!

TO RALLY THE FLAGGING SPIRITS OF THE MEN, ODYSSEUS ORDERS AN ELABORATE FUNERAL TO BE STAGED, WITH SEVENTEEN DAYS OF FUNERAL GAMES TO HONOR ACHILLES' MEMORY.

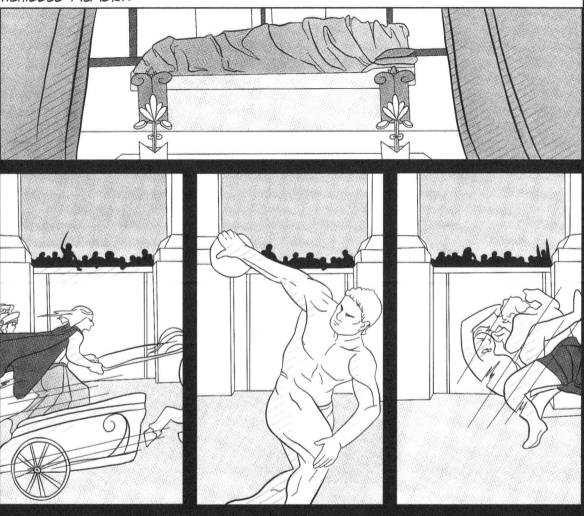

TERRIFIED AT THE THOUGHT OF LOSING THE WAR, AGAMEMNON SETS THE SHREWD KING OF ITHACA TO THE MOST DIFFICULT TASK HE'S EVER GIVEN HIM.

IF YOU EVER WANT TO SEE THE SHORES OF ITHACA AGAIN, GET US INSIDE THAT CITY— I DON'T CARE HOW! YOU HAVE SEVENTEEN DAYS TO FIGURE IT OUT, AND THEN WE ATTACK. BY YOUR CUNNING, EITHER WE DIE AT THE WALLS, OR WE TAKE TROY.

CHAPTER TWELVE

GÖTTERDÄMMERUNG

AS ACHILLES' FUNERAL GAMES CONTINUED, ODYSSEUS SCHEMED. FEARING AGAMEMNON'S WRATH AND GROWING INCREASINGLY WORRIED THAT HE MIGHT NEVER RETURN TO ITHACA, ODYSSEUS REALIZED THAT THE TEN YEARS ALREADY SPENT IN A FUTILE SIEGE MEANT THAT TROY WOULD HAVE TO BE TAKEN BY UNCONVENTIONAL MEANS.

PLEASE ATHENA, WISE, WARRIOR-VIRGIN, SEND ME GUIDANCE IN MY DREAMS. I MUST GET HOME TO MY WIFE AND SON.

THAT NIGHT, ODYSSEUS DREAMED NOT OF THE WARRIOR MAIDEN, BUT WAS INSTEAD VISITED BY ACHILLES' SHADE.

WAKING FROM HIS FITFUL SLEEP, ODYSSEUS SITS BY THE RIVER SCAMANDER, AND PONDERS THE MEANING OF ACHILLES' STRANGE RIDDLE.

NO FRUIT GROWS ON THE BARREN PLAINS OF NORTHERN GREECE... WHAT DOES HE MEAN?

ATHENA HAS SENT ME WITH THIS MESSAGE: WHEN TROY ACCEPTS THE GREEKS' GIFTS AND THEIR RECKLESS HUNGER LEADS THEM TO DINE ON THE FINEST FRUITS OF THE PLAINS OF THESSALY, *ONLY* THEN WILL TROY FALL.

173

ODYSSEUS TAKES THE GREEK HORSES TO THE RIVER. THE ROTTING BODIES OF THE COMMON SOLDIERS STILL LITTER THE AREA, POLLUTING THE WATER AND AIR WITH DEATH AND DISEASE.

GIVE THEM A GOOD LONG DRINK.

I CAN'T BELIEVE WE'RE DOING THIS... THIS IS MADNESS.

I'M SORRY...

ODYSSEUS BEGINS TO PUT HIS PLAN INTO MOTION. FIRST, HE ENLISTS THE SERVICE OF SINON, HIS MOST TRUSTED AGENT.

SINON, I HAVE A FINAL MISSION FOR YOU. DELIVER THESE HORSES TO TROY, AND ANNOUNCE TO THE TROJANS THAT WE HAVE GIVEN UP. TELL THEM ATHENA ORDERED US TO OFFER THESE HORSES AS PAYMENT FOR THE SINS WE HAVE COMMITTED IN HER NAME SO THAT SHE WILL PROTECT US ON OUR JOURNEY HOME. YOU UNDERSTAND WHAT THIS MIGHT MEAN FOR YOU?

I DO.

NO PLEASE, I BEG YOU!

GODS, GIVE ME THE STRENGTH TO KEEP MY PROMISE AND KEEP ODYSSEUS' SECRET.

THE CRIES OF SINON ECHO UP FROM THE TORTURE CHAMBER, BUT NO MATTER WHAT HORRORS ARE INFLICTED UPON HIM, HE REFUSES TO BETRAY HIS FELLOW GREEKS. WHEN THE GREEK FLEET IS SEEN TO SAIL AWAY, THE TROJANS FATEFULLY BELIEVE THE WAR IS TRULY OVER AND THAT IT IS TIME TO REJOICE.

THE TROJAN PEOPLE ASSEMBLE IN THE GREAT COURTYARD. DRIVEN BY NECESSITY AND HUNGER, PRIAM ORDERS THE HORSES TO BE BUTCHERED AND DISTRIBUTED TO MASSES IN A GREAT BANQUET TO CELEBRATE THE END OF THE LONG WAR. A FESTIVE MOOD BEGINS TO PERMEATE THE CITY. DANCING, MUSIC, DRINKING, AND THE SOUNDS OF JOY, UNHEARD FOR MANY YEARS, ONCE AGAIN RING OUT IN THE STREETS OF TROY. THOUGHTS OF WAR ARE SOON ABANDONED, AND EVEN SOLDIERS TURN INTO REVELERS.

BUT NOT EVEN THE GODS COULD SPARE THE TROJANS FROM WHAT FATE HAD IN STORE FOR THEM. THE CRIES OF JOY THAT FILLED THE STREETS SOON TURNED TO WAILS OF DESPAIR. FOR, SHORTLY AFTER THE BANQUET, THOSE WHO DINED ON THE PLAGUE-INFESTED HORSEFLESH, DISGUISED AS A PEACE OFFERING, BEGAN GETTING SICK AND DYING IN GREAT NUMBERS. AS DISEASE RAVAGED THE CITY, ORDER DESCENDED INTO MADNESS, AND IN THEIR DESPERATE ATTEMPTS TO SURVIVE, MANY TROJANS BROKE OPEN THEIR OWN MIGHTY GATES AND FLED INTO THE COUNTRYSIDE, LEAVING THE GREAT CITY DEFENSELESS AND NEARLY ABANDONED.

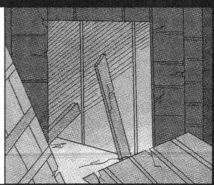

DOGS AND JACKALS WANDER THE STREETS, FEASTING ON THE CORPSES TOO NUMEROUS TO BURY. HOW DID THIS COME TO BE? IT WAS, OF COURSE, ODYSSEUS' GIFT.

NOT HAVING JOINED THE MASSES IN EATING THE HORSE MEAT, THE ROYAL FAMILY AND THEIR ENTOURAGE DID NOT SUCCUMB TO THE PLAGUE THAT KILLED MANY TROJANS. THEY, ALONG WITH MANY OF THE SCATTERED SURVIVORS, TRY AND MAKE SENSE OF THE CRISIS IN THE CRUMBLING CITY.

MEANWHILE, FROM THE HEIGHTS OF THE ISLAND OF TENEDOS, BEHIND WHICH THE GREEK FLEET HAS BEEN LYING HIDDEN SINCE FEIGNING RETREAT FROM THE BEACHES OF TROY, ODYSSEUS SEES SMOKE RISING FROM TROY IN THE DISTANCE. HE REALIZES HIS PLAN HAS WORKED AND THE CITY LIES OPEN.

YOUR PRIZE IS READY FOR THE TAKING.

ORDER THE SHIP CAPTAINS TO RUN UP THE RED FLAGS—THE RED FLAGS OF SLAUGHTER. THERE WILL BE NO MERCY. THERE WILL BE NO QUARTER. BY SUNSET, TROY WILL BE BUT A MEMORY. I WILL WASH AWAY IPHIGENIA'S SACRIFICE WITH THE BLOOD OF PRIAM'S CHILDREN.

THE MEAGER DEFENSE PUT UP BY THE TROJANS, THOUGH BRAVE, OFFERS LITTLE RESISTANCE TO THE REMORSELESS GREEKS WHO ARE FILLED WITH LUST FOR SLAUGHTER.

THE PALACE GUARDS FIGHT A BRAVE BUT LOSING BATTLE. THE GREEKS QUICKLY SPREAD THROUGHOUT THE TROJAN STRONGHOLD. DEIPHOBUS, TERRIBLY WOUNDED, FIGHTS ON, INSPIRING THE LAST OF TROY'S SOLDIERS AND PARIS, WITH HIS BOW, TO DO LIKEWISE.

FOR ACHILLES!

FOR MENELAUS AND SPARTA!

FOR HECTOR AND TROY!

AAAAAAHHHHH

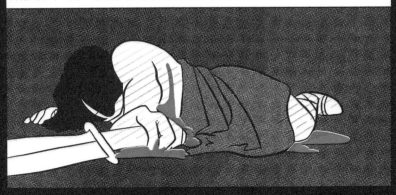

DESPITE PARIS' NOBLE INTENTIONS, HE WAS NO MATCH FOR THE BATTLE-HARDENED GREEK SOLDIERS.

DEIPHOBUS DIES, THOUGH, SHORTLY AFTER HE BEGS HELEN TO LEAVE, UNABLE TO PREVENT HIS BELOVED CITY'S FALL. HIS PURSUERS CAN BE HEARD NOT FAR BEHIND.

GET OUT, HELEN. PARIS IS DEAD. ANDROMACHE AND ASTYANAX HAVE BEEN CAPTURED. THE GREEKS AREN'T FAR BEHIND ME— GO!

DEIPHOBUS... YOU WERE TRUE TO YOUR OATH AND DIED BEFORE THE CITY FELL... I'M SORRY FOR ALL THAT HAS BEEN BROUGHT UPON YOUR FAMILY AND PEOPLE.

A FEW MOMENTS LATER, MENELAUS ARRIVES IN SEARCH OF HIS WIFE, HAVING LEARNED OF HER ROOM'S LOCATION FROM A TERRIFIED TROJAN SERVANT.

HMMM... EVEN AFTER ALL THIS TIME, SHE'S STILL AS BEAUTIFUL AS THE DAY WE MET. PITY I'M GOING TO KILL HER.

THERE YOU ARE, FAITHLESS WIFE...

...STILL THINK YOUR BEAUTY WILL SAVE YOU?

STAY WHERE YOU ARE, GOOD KING AND HUSBAND. ALLOW ME A MOMENT TO SLIP INTO SOMETHING MORE APPROPRIATE.

I HAVE OTHER STRENGTHS NOW.

KEEP LOOKING, YOU OLD FOOL.

YES— STILL THE MOST BEAUTIFUL WOMAN IN THE LAND, BUT SHE HUMILIATED ME ALL THE SAME.

I'M NOT THE SAME WOMAN WHO FLED SPARTA.

WHAT IS SHE DOING BACK THERE? IT LOOKS LIKE SHE'S PUTTING ON...

ARMOR?! WHAT ARE YOU WEARING THAT FOR? YOU'RE NOT A MAN!

YOU'RE DAMN RIGHT. I'M AN AMAZON!

AFTER MENELAUS' AND HELEN'S "REUNION," SPARTAN SOLDIERS ARRIVE TO FIND THEIR KING "REUNITED" WITH HIS STOLEN BRIDE. THE SOLDIERS ARE CONFUSED BY WHAT THEY SEE, MENELAUS AND HELEN TOGETHER, SEEMINGLY HAPPY.

KING MENELAUS, ARE YOU ALRIGHT?

WHY WOULDN'T I BE— *I'VE* FOUND THE QUEEN. MAKE READY FOR US TO RETURN TO THE SHIPS. I'VE GOT WHAT I CAME FOR.

BUT LORD, WE'LL MISS OUT ON THE LOOTING.

NOW! WE'RE GOING BACK TO THE SHIPS.

YES, MY KING.

THE GREEKS GIVE IN TO THEIR FURY AND RESENTMENT AND SACK THE CITY MERCILESSLY FOR A DAY AND A NIGHT. MUCH OF THE CITY IS BURNING OR DESTROYED, AND CRIES OF TERROR AND PAIN FILL THE NIGHT SKY.

THROUGH THE SMOKE AND SHADOWS, THE IMAGE OF A SLAUGHTERED HORSE MAKES THE SCENE EVEN MORE MACABRE—A GRIZZLY AND PERMANENT MEMORY FOR ALL WHO WITNESSED THE HORROR. LATER, WHEN SURVIVORS TOLD THE STORY OF TROY'S FALL AND IT WAS PASSED THROUGH GENERATIONS, IT WAS FROM A SCENE LIKE THIS THAT THE LEGEND OF THE TROJAN HORSE WOULD EVOLVE.

THOSE FEW TROJANS INSIDE THE CITY, LUCKY ENOUGH TO SURVIVE THE MADNESS OF THE SACK, ARE ROUNDED UP TO BE TAKEN BACK TO THE GREEK KINGDOMS AS SLAVES. IN CAPTIVITY, THEY WOULD QUESTION WHETHER IT WAS THE LUCKY ONES WHO DIED DURING THE SIEGE.

AS THE NEXT DAY BREAKS AND THE GREEKS LOOK AROUND, THEY BEGIN TO COMPREHEND THE DEPRAVITY OF THEIR ACTIONS.

GREAT AJAX OF THE MIGHTY SHIELD— DID WE GREEKS REALLY DO THIS?

BY THE GODS, IT WAS US. BUT THIS ISN'T WAR. WHAT WE DID HAS NOTHING TO DO WITH BATTLE OR HONOR. WE'VE CURSED OURSELVES.

AS AJAX CONTEMPLATES THE COST OF WAR, ODYSSEUS THINKS ONLY OF ITHACA AND HIS FAMILY.

I'M GOING HOME. YOU GOT YOUR VICTORY, AGAMEMNON. I HOPE YOU CAN LIVE WITH IT.

AS THE SACK OF THE CITY CONTINUES, AGAMEMNON BEGINS TO SEARCH FOR TROY'S GREAT TREASURES. TWO WRETCHED OLD TROJANS, THINKING ONLY OF THEIR OWN LIVES AND CARING NOTHING FOR THE FUTURE, BETRAY THE PROMISES THEY HAD MADE TO NOBLE HECTOR TO SAFEGUARD THE CITY'S WEALTH AND SEEK A TREACHEROUS AUDIENCE WITH AGAMEMNON.

TROY'S WEALTH IS MINE.

GUARDS! BRING ME THOSE TWO TROJAN TRAITORS.

SOME THINGS NEVER CHANGE. FEAR ALWAYS DRAWS THE BIGGEST RATS OUT OF THE SEWER. THANKS FOR HANDING OVER THE WEALTH OF TROY. I'LL SEE TO IT THAT YOU GET A "TRAITOR'S REWARD." GUARDS—TAKE THIS SCUM AWAY.

NOOOOOOO!

EVEN MT OLYMPUS, WHERE THE WAR HAD BEGUN WITH ZEUS' DISAFFECTION WITH HUMANITY, HAD NOT ESCAPED THE WAR'S REACH AND IMPACT. EVEN THE MIGHTY GODS WERE NOT IMMUNE TO THE CONSEQUENCES OF THE CONFLICT: THEIR LUSTER WAS DIMINISHED, AND THEY HAD BEGUN TO AGE! SOON, EVEN THEY WOULD BE CASUALTIES OF THE WAR THEY HAD CALLOUSLY SUPPORTED.

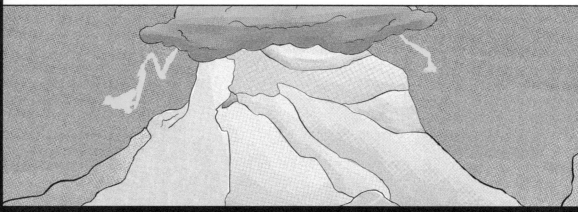

NOW LARGELY IGNORED BY THOSE MORTALS WHO HAVE BEEN CONSUMED WITH THE SUFFERING OF WAR, THE GODS' POWERS HAVE BEGUN TO WANE. EVEN IN THEIR DIMINISHED STATE, THEY CONTINUED TO FIGHT AND SQUABBLE, SEEMINGLY OBLIVIOUS TO THE TWILIGHT OF THEIR OWN REIGN.

AGAMEMNON COMES TO SEE THE KING OF ITHACA AS HE PREPARES TO DEPART FOR HOME. WITH THE TASTE OF VICTORY STILL FRESH IN HIS MOUTH AND REJOICING IN THE LAMENTATIONS OF THE MOURNERS, AGAMEMNON IS CONFIDENT THAT HIS NAME WILL LIVE ON IN MEMORY AS A GREAT CONQUEROR.

AT THE PACE YOUR MEN MOVE, ODYSSEUS, YOU'LL BE THE FIRST TO LEAVE. WE HAVEN'T EVEN DIVIDED ALL THE SPOILS! STAY. EMBRACE THIS MOMENT!

I'VE BEEN AWAY FROM HOME FOR TOO LONG. WE ALL HAVE. WE SHOULD MAKE OUR SACRIFICES AND DEPART FROM THIS PLACE. WHO KNOWS WHAT'S GONE ON BACK HOME IN OUR ABSENCE?

YOU WORRY TOO MUCH. WE ACHIEVED A GREAT VICTORY HERE. A VICTORY FOR ALL OF GREECE! IN A SHORT TIME, WE'LL BE ON FAMILIAR SHORES, HAILED AS THE HEROES WE ARE.

AS YOU SAY, *AGAMEMNON.*

I REMEMBER WHEN YOU ADDRESSED ME AS "MY LORD."

I DID A LOT OF THINGS I FOUND PARTICULARLY UNSAVORY TO END THIS WAR AND GET HOME.

YOU'RE A CLEVER ONE WITH WORDS, ODYSSEUS... TOO CLEVER. DID YOU HEAR? MY BROTHER DECIDED TO TAKE HELEN BACK TO SPARTA AS HIS QUEEN. CAN YOU BELIEVE IT? ALMOST AS IF THIS WAR WAS ALL FOR NOTHING. HA!

DON'T WORRY, AGAMEMNON. EVERY COMMON SOLIDER KNOWS WHAT THIS WAR WAS ABOUT: THEY'RE THE ONLY ONES WHO DO. LET PEOPLE SAY WE FOUGHT FOR HELEN. I DON'T GIVE A DAMN. I FOUGHT TO GET HOME ALIVE.

AS ODYSSEUS' SHIP DISAPPEARS OVER THE HORIZON, AGAMEMNON TURNS TO WALK BACK TO THE SMOLDERING REMAINS OF TROY TO PREPARE FOR HIS RETURN TO MYCENAE AND HIS WIFE CLYTEMNESTRA. HIS PATH WILL TAKE HIM THROUGH THE FORMER FIELDS OF BATTLE WHERE COUNTLESS SOLDIERS AND HEROES SHED THEIR BLOOD. ACROSS THE DUSTY AND RUINED LANDSCAPE, SIGNS OF RENEWAL AND REBIRTH ARE SEEN EVERYWHERE. BRIGHT RED PATCHES OF POPPIES GROW WHERE ONCE POOLS OF BLOOD HAD PROVIDED THE ONLY COLOR ON THE BLEAK AND JOYLESS LANDSCAPE.

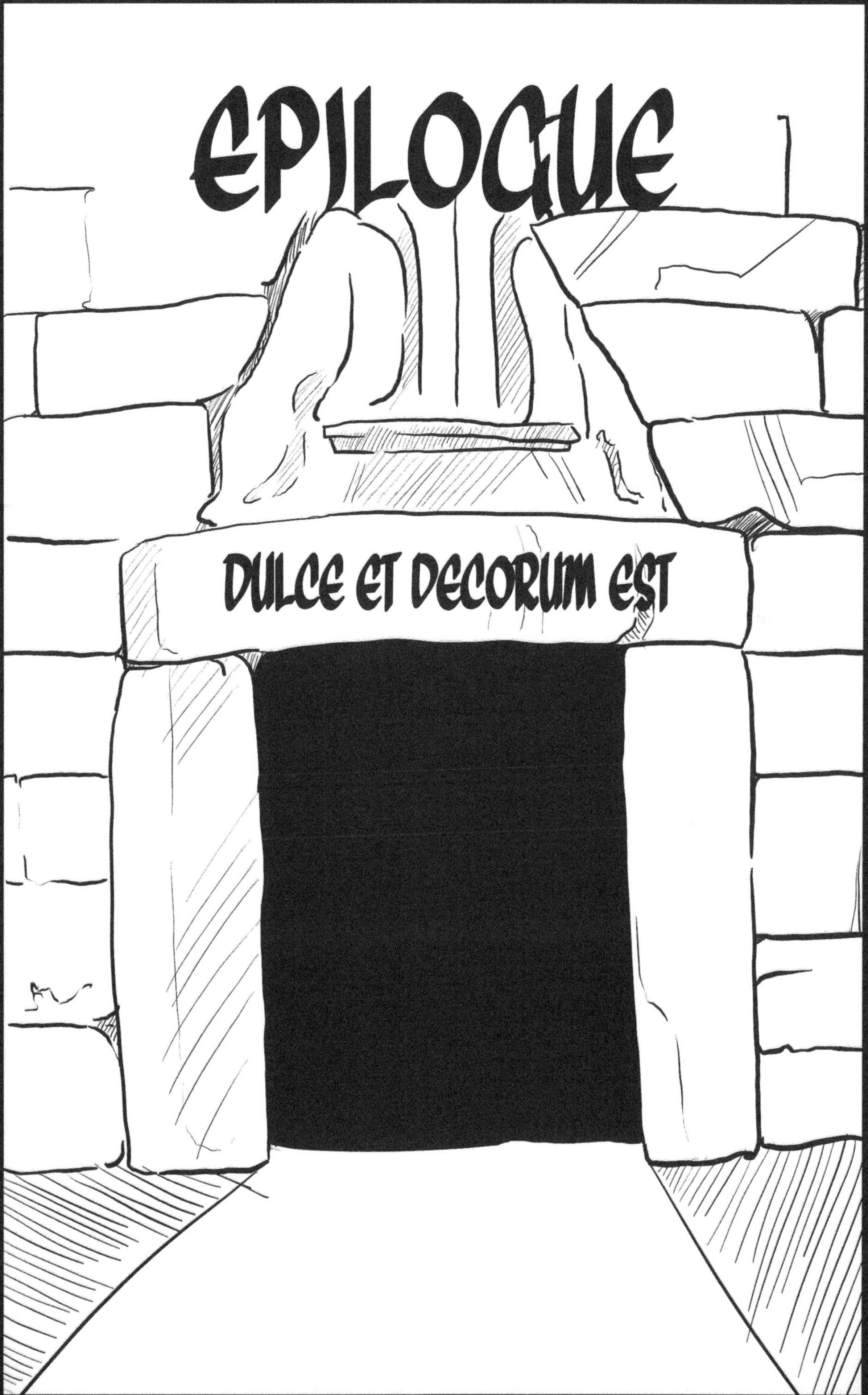
EPILOGUE
DULCE ET DECORUM EST

AS ARISTOTLE WOULD LATER SAY, EVERY STORY HAS A BEGINNING, MIDDLE, AND END. BUT AS WE KNOW, NO STORY IS EVER TRULY OVER.

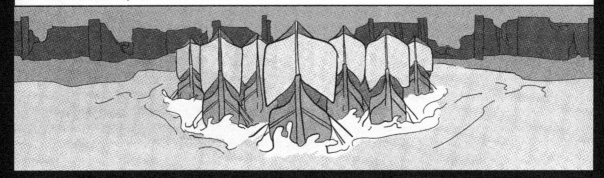

UPON HIS RETURN TO MYCENAE, AGAMEMNON WAS "GREETED" BY HIS WIFE CLYTEMNESTRA, WHO HAD NOT FORGOTTEN THE SACRIFICE OF THEIR DAUGHTER IPHIGENIA.

WHILE AGAMEMNON SAT IN HIS ROYAL BATH, SURROUNDED BY CONCUBINES HE HAD BROUGHT HOME FROM TROY...

I HAVE RETURNED! OUR TREASURY OVERFLOWS! BEHOLD WOMAN—I AM THE KING OF KINGS!

... CLYTEMNESTRA EXACTED HER REVENGE FOR WHAT AGAMEMNON DID TO THEIR DAUGHTER. HER MURDER OF AGAMEMNON WOULD INSPIRE AESCHYLUS IN THE 5TH CENTURY BC TO IMMORTALIZE HER VIOLENT REPRISAL IN A SERIES OF TRAGEDIES WRITTEN FOR THE ATHENIAN STAGE.

THE MIGHTY AJAX, TORMENTED BY WHAT HE WITNESSED AT TROY, FOUND THAT BEING BACK HOME BROUGHT HIM NO JOY. HIS MOODS WERE ILL. HE HAD TROUBLE SLEEPING, AND HE BECAME INCREASINGLY SUSPICIOUS OF OTHERS, WITHDRAWING FROM EVERYONE AROUND HIM.

MORE AND MORE, THE MIGHTY WARRIOR, HAILED AS A HERO, HEARD AND SAW THINGS THAT WEREN'T THERE. ONE DAY, IN A DRUNKEN RAGE, HE ATTACKED AND SLAUGHTERED A HERD OF SHEEP, BELIEVING THEY WERE TROJANS COMING TO TAKE THEIR REVENGE. WHEN HE CAME TO HIS SENSES AND SAW WHAT HE'D DONE, HE WENT MAD WITH GRIEF AND RAGE AND TOOK HIS OWN LIFE.

COUNTLESS GREEK SOLDIERS, LUCKY ENOUGH TO SURVIVE THE WAR, RETURNED HOME TO UNCERTAIN FUTURES. SOME WERE REVILED—EVEN BY THEIR FELLOW GREEKS. MANY HAD DIFFICULTY RETURNING TO THEIR FORMER LIVES. LIKE AJAX, THEIR DAYS AT TROY HAUNTED THEM IN THEIR WAKING AND SLEEPING HOURS.

OTHERS, LIKE THE BRAVE EURYTUS, UNABLE TO LIVE WITH THE BURDEN OF SURVIVING, SIMPLY GAVE UP. THEY CHOSE TO FORGET, PARTAKING OF THE LOTUS TO CLOUD THEIR MINDS.

A LUCKY FEW, SUCH AS HOMER, FOUND PEACE AND EVEN WELL INTO THE TWILIGHT YEARS OF HIS LIFE, REGALED ANYONE WHO WOULD LISTEN WITH FIRSTHAND ACCOUNTS OF HIS STORIES FROM TROY—STORIES WHICH BECAME TALES, WHICH EVENTUALLY BECAME LEGENDS.

IT WAS WILY ODYSSEUS WHO TRICKED THE TROJANS WITH THE GIFT OF A HORSE—A HORSE WITH SOMETHING DEADLY INSIDE.

197

ANDROMACHE WAS GIVEN AS A WAR-PRIZE TO THE MYRMIDON CAPTAIN, NEOPTOLEMUS. AS SHE WAS LED INTO CAPTIVITY, SHE WALKED SOLEMNLY PAST THE BODIES OF SLAIN TROJAN CHILDREN, TOSSED MERCILESSLY FROM THE WALLS OF TROY FOR THE AMUSEMENT OF GREEK SOLDIERS. AMONGST THE PILE OF BROKEN BODIES, SHE SAW HER OWN LITTLE SON. IN THAT MOMENT SHE KNEW AN ANCIENT TRUTH: WAR IS HATEFUL TO MOTHERS.

THE GREEKS KILLED MANY TROJANS ON THAT FINAL DAY OF THE WAR, BUT NOT ALL OF THEM. AENEAS, BELOVED SON OF APHRODITE, LED A GROUP OF REFUGEES AWAY FROM TROY IN SEARCH OF A NEW HOMELAND.

AENEAS AND HIS COMPANIONS TRAVELED FOR SOME TIME, FACED MANY DANGERS AND EVENTUALLY SETTLED IN A NEW LAND WHERE THEY WERE WELCOMED BY THE LOCAL PEOPLE—THE LATINS. THERE, MANY CENTURIES LATER ONE OF AENEAS' DESCENDANTS WOULD FOUND A CITY IN THE SHADOW OF SEVEN HILLS.

IN THE FUTURE, THESE PEOPLE—THE ROMANS— WOULD COME BACK TO HAUNT THE GREEKS.

OF ALL THE GREEK KINGS, ODYSSEUS WAS MOST EAGER TO RETURN HOME. HOWEVER, HIS CONDUCT DURING THE WAR BROUGHT HIM UNWANTED ATTENTION FROM THE GODS. DISPLEASED WITH ODYSSEUS' WILLINGNESS TO BREAK SACRED OATHS, POSEIDON, ON BEHALF OF THE GODS, UNLEASHED A TERRIBLE STORM TO THROW HIM OFF COURSE. THE KING OF ITHACA WOULD GO ON TO SUFFER MANY OTHER SETBACKS.

THE GODS ARE PUNISHING ME, MY LOYAL FRIEND. THE DEAD COME TO ME IN MY SLEEP. THE CRIES OF THE DYING NEVER CEASE IN MY EARS. THE SMELL OF THAT PLACE HAUNTS ME. WHEN WILL IT END FOR ME?

NO! I *WILL* GET HOME!

ODYSSEUS WOULDN'T ARRIVE BACK TO THE SHORES OF ITHACA FOR ANOTHER TEN YEARS.

MY NAME IS "NOBODY."

I'M THE GODDESS CALYPSO, AND I'LL TAKE WHAT I WANT: ODYSSEUS SHALL BE MY IMMORTAL HUSBAND.

I'M STUCK IN HELL!

HELEN AND MENELAUS RETURNED TO SPARTA WITHOUT FURTHER INCIDENT. THERE, SHE ASSUMED THE ROYAL DUTIES AND RULED AS A WARRIOR-QUEEN. IN THE FUTURE, SPARTAN WOMEN WOULD CONTINUE HELEN'S POWERFUL LEGACY.

YEARS LATER, TELEMACHUS, ODYSSEUS' SON, CAME TO SPARTA IN SEARCH OF HIS FATHER WHO HAD MYSTERIOUSLY YET TO RETURN FROM THE WAR. HELEN SPOKE WITH HIM AT LENGTH ABOUT HER TIME AT TROY.

SO, THE WAR WASN'T ABOUT YOU?

NO... NO, IT WASN'T. IT WAS ABOUT THE GREED OF MEN AND THEIR LUST FOR POWER. ALL THAT REMAINS OF THAT ONCE GREAT CITY ARE TINY RED FLOWERS... I'LL ALWAYS REMEMBER THOSE POPPIES...

CHARACTER	EPITHET	PG REF
Achilles	"Breaker of men"	69
	"Lion-hearted Achilles"	71
	"Son of Peleus"	x
	"Fights like a lion"	106
	"Like a god" / "god-like"	97 / 157
	"Goddess-born Achilles"	124
	"Noble Achilles"	147
	"Swift-footed"	152
Agamemnon	"Lord of men"	64 / 145
Ajax	"Ajax the Great"	xi
	"Great Ajax of the Mighty Shield"	190
	"Ajax of the towering shield"	121
	"Mighty Ajax"	197
Amazons	"Proud Amazons"	108
Aphrodite	"Daughter of Zeus"	vi
	"Goddess of Love"	vi / 13 / 32
Apollo	"Son of Zeus"	viii
Artemis	"Goddess of the hunt"	vi / 77
Athena	"Grey-eyed Athena"	111
	"Daughter of Zeus"	vi
Greeks	"Long-haired"	123
Hector	"The man-slayer" / "man-killing"	xiii / 92 / 157
	"Horse-tamer"	124
	"Reaper of men"	142
Hermes	"Messenger of the gods"	vii / 16
Hephaestus	"Master of the forge"	149
Odysseus	"Wily" / "Ever-wily Odysseus"	174 / 197
	"Cunning"	ix
	"Courageous"	67
	"King of Ithaca"	67 / 148 / 193
	"Wily king of Ithaca" / "Shrewd King of Ithaca"	122 / 171
	"Master of cunning and spies"	144
	"Silver tongued"	150
	"Sly Odysseus"	176

Continued

CHARACTER	EPITHET	PG REF
Palamedes	"Loyal Palamedes"	64
Zeus	"The thunderer"	31
	"Lord of the oak"	66
	"The cloud-crasher"	90
	"All-powerful"	45
	"Lord of the sky"	75